Barfly

What Growing up in a Taproom Taught Me about Life, Death, and Ever After

Catherine DePino

Published by Rogue Phoenix Press, LLP
Copyright © 2025

ISBN: 978-1-62420-866-9

Editor: Amanda Armstrong

Cover Artist: Designs by Ms G

Dedication
To my family for all
they've taught me.

Acknowledgments

Thanks to Christine and Arlo for giving me the chance to tell my story. Thanks to Genene Valleau, artist and writer, for making my story come to life by using powerful photos on the cover. Thanks to my readers. I hope you take away something positive from my book.

Chapter One
All Couples Fight

"Someday I'll write a Story about All the Characters in the Bar "
—Joe the Bartender, AKA. Dad"

From the time I was a toddler until I turned eleven, I lived in a spacious apartment above The Royal Gardens Restaurant and Bar in Bensalem, PA, a suburb of Philadelphia. My family's business seemed set apart from the world, located across the street from the Roosevelt Jewish Cemetery and bordered by the Lincoln Highway, a perilous speedway where cars sped by like lightening all hours of the day and night. If you walked along that highway, you were asking for trouble.

Sometimes I thought I heard the people in the cemetery calling out to me at night. They mostly said stuff like, "Don't be sad for us. Things are better where we are now and much easier, so don't be afraid of life, death, and ever after. It's all good." Was I hearing voices, or were their visitations a precursor of my interest in the unseen world and psychic phenomena, like Tarot, angel cards and Reiki healing?

When I attended Our Lady of Grace School, I'd learned about Saint Joan of Arc, who heard voices, but I definitely wasn't in that category. Maybe I'd inherited Dad's mental problems. Whatever it was, I kept the voices to myself, or Mom would have had my head examined by one of the psychiatrists who trekked to their favorite taproom every day after their harrowing shifts at Byberry Mental Hospital, the area's main landmark.

Most kids who grew up in Philly or on the outskirts lived in smacked-together brick-front row homes or sprawling ranch houses on tree-lined streets in the suburbs, where they played ball and horsed around with kids their age. I lived on a dangerous highway, so parents hesitated to bring their kids over for playdates or sleepovers for fear they might get hurt or killed.

My friends were mainly the people who worked at The Royal Gardens, like Miss Laura, the cleaning lady, and Miss Clara, the waitress. My other friends were the psychiatrists and attendants at Byberry Hospital who visited the bar every day. Once in a while, a patient slipped in, but few people noticed the difference. Usually they were funny, and we had some good conversations. That's okay because all these people were better friends than kids sometimes.

Before moving to the Royal Gardens, we lived in army housing in Miami Beach, Florida. My dad, whom everyone called "Joe the Bartender," although his baptismal name was Emidio Joseph, was an army officer who worked as a supervisor in the army mess hall, where the servicemen and women ate.

Dad, whose first language was Italian, excelled in school and loved Latin and Greek. He graduated from the University of Pennsylvania and majored in law. He ended up running The Royal Gardens restaurant and bar because he suffered from depression and anxiety that doctors later diagnosed as bi-polar disorder, then called manic-depression. No one knew, except his family. He was great at hiding it.

Pop Pop, my grandfather, who owned a farm down the road and sold his wares, like lettuce, tomatoes, corn, and strawberries, from the back of his pick-up truck, said it would be best for Dad if he set him up in a business; in this case, as a proprietor of a restaurant and bar. A job like lawyer or professor might trigger serious depressive and anxiety attacks, "Make-a-him go to Byberry Hospital" was the way Pop Pop put it in broken English, tapping his head twice with his index finger for emphasis. He would do anything for his kids, so there was no question he'd look out for Dad.

An enormous red, white, and green Royal Gardens sign swung back and forth outside my bedroom window in the apartment above the bar in a clangy, trochaic rhythm. *Whee, woo, whee woo*, it sang all through the night into the wee hours of the morning, lulling me into a dreamless sleep (except for my frequent visits from the dead in Roosevelt Cemetery) until it was time to wake up at seven a.m.

That's when my mom, Mary Grace, the cook, server, and main troubleshooter, ambled downstairs in her white uniform and hairnet to prep the food in the restaurant for its 11 o'clock opening. Every morning, Mom cooked a breakfast of sausage, scrambled eggs, and coffee for her and Dad, and cinnamon toast with hot chocolate and marshmallows for me.

My mom, known as Grace, was billed a top student at Eastern High, an academic high school in Baltimore, Maryland. She wanted to attend college and become an interpreter for the United Nations. She had stunning classic looks: wavy brown hair, huge almond-shaped brown eyes, and all the guys loved her. Mom's main interest was going to college and having a successful career. Marriage could wait, or so she thought.

Back in the day as was the custom, her family sent the boys to college, rather than the girls. She had two brothers, Joe and Nick. Joe sold cars and eventually opened his own business, becoming one of the most successful car dealers on the east coast. His brother Nick served **in the Navy** and eventually became an engineer after graduating from Johns Hopkins and MIT and became vice-president and general manager at Lockheed Martin.

Mom's family all came from Baltimore, Maryland. Mom had three sisters, and they were all best friends. Aunt Diana, the oldest, got married later in life, and had six kids after age 40. She started her own successful elder care business, and her husband became a happy househusband while she grew her business.

She was a liberated woman before her time, walking in the footsteps of Betty Friedan and Gloria Steinem. Her sister, Marguerite, grew orchids and sold them from her greenhouse for weddings and other celebrations, while the youngest, Monica, worked her way from teacher to superintendent of Palm Beach County Schools, and she also raised three kids. Monica was born when they were all grown up.

Mom's family was a high-achieving family, so Mom wanted to imitate her sisters and have a professional job in addition to raising a family, but it didn't happen for her after she met my dad. Everyone thought that my mom would have a successful career, and in a way she did. Being the co-boss, cook, waitress, and occasional bartender at The Royal Gardens wasn't in her plans although she made the best of it.

When Mom was eighteen, she worked as a head secretary for the military. She met my dad when they worked in the same office where he was a second lieutenant, and she worked as a secretary. It was love at first sight for both of them. Dad was Mom's boss at the base, and she found his Latin looks and outgoing personality charming and irresistible, just as he loved her quiet ways and shy, endearing smile. In less than six months, they got engaged and married in a nuptial mass with bridesmaids, ushers, and baskets of gardenias and roses, Mom's favorite flowers.

Mom loved to tell us stories about their courtship. "He'd buy me a nickel Coke and try to squeeze it out of me on our dates, but that's as far as it went." It was important to her as a good Catholic girl to save herself for marriage.

She didn't know how to cook when she married Dad but decided to become the restaurant's chef when Fred, the cook, and the dismal procession that followed, dipped their ladles into the spaghetti sauce and slurped a generous swig of the fragrant tomato gravy, which is what they call it in South Philly, heavy with the scents of fresh rosemary and garlic.

"Um-umm," or "delish," the cooks proclaimed when sampling their culinary creations, dumping their spoons and slimy saliva back into the pot. Mom cringed and told them to stop, or the board of health would come after us, but they never did.

"That's why it tastes so good, Miss Grace," Fred the cook told her, smiling widely. "A little spit never hurt anyone."

She and Dad decided they had to do something about the spoon-licking, so they fired the cooks, one by one. What would their customers say if they knew? It was bad enough that Mom and Dad knew. Luckily, Mom watched the chefs prepare comfort food specialties, such as lasagna, roast turkey, rib roast, and crispy steak fries (the secret was in the blanching process). She knew how to make all her customers' favorites, and she began to add new touches of her own. Customers raved about her specialties even more than those of Fred, the cook, and the other chefs. She was a natural. People craved Mom's cooking and traveled miles to sample it.

Mom expertly prepared lasagna, meat loaf, roast beef, savory soups, and desserts like her orange cake, for her customers, just as she would for her family. My parents hosted huge dinners for the Lions and Kiwanis clubs as well as small, intimate suppers for couples, along with family dinners, in their spacious dining room for anniversaries and birthdays. People always asked for her recipes, which I have included in the appendix of this book, and she willingly shared them. "I'll never understand why people don't want to divulge their recipes," Mom said once. "I consider it the highest compliment and want everyone to enjoy them and pass them on to others." Mom was always generous to others, and we found it always came back to her in good ways.

Every morning, except for Sunday when we closed, Miss Laura, the cleaning lady, let herself in after getting her kids off to school and walking a mile to work. Dad always picked her up in bad weather. One morning she shook her head when she saw Dad stocking the bar. "Mr. Joe, you'd better tell those guys who use the bathroom to aim straight when they pee. I'm sick of cleaning up their stinky mess."

"Good luck with that," Dad said with a smile.

But Miss Laura wouldn't be put off because she always got the last word. "I'm serious, Mr. Joe. Either say something or you won't see Miss Laura come Monday. I'll get a job on the cleaning crew at the Holiday Inn down the road. I've got connections there. They already offered me a job with benefits, in case you didn't know."

"We certainly wouldn't want to lose you to The Holiday Inn," Mom said. "Besides, I don't think you'd like it there. I heard they have nasty bed bugs that latch on to you and leave you itching all day."

"For real?" Miss Laura flashed her dark eyes at Mom. "You know I love you, Miss Grace, but I can tell when you're lying."

"How's that, Miss Laura?"

"Your face gets blotchy red, and your nose grows like Pinocchio's."

Mom rolled her eyes and turned to Dad. "Do something, Joe. We can't afford to lose our best employee."

Dad shot Miss Laura a somber look. "Okay, then. I'll give those guys the word about peeing straight into the pot if you promise not to leave."

Miss Laura dipped her mop in the bucket and sloshed it around in the soapy water, splashing Dad in the process, probably on purpose. "Aww, you know I'd never leave, Mr. Joe. Besides, I love Catherine. I enjoy hearing her funny stories about those shrinks and attendants at Byberry Mental Hospital, although it seems to me that a few of them act a lot like the patients who sneak in here sometimes. Most of all, I love that Elvis music she plays on the jukebox. We both predicted "Heartbreak Hotel" would be a big hit and it was. We're a team, you know."

I ran to Miss Laura, and she hugged me so hard I could hear my bones creak, but she was my friend so that was fine, and we told each other secrets and laughed at the characters at the bar behind their backs, so I didn't say anything.

Shortly before Dad died, he told me that someday he'd write about all the characters in the bar. He never got around to it, so I guess I'm the one to tell what it was like living at The Royal Gardens. However, my story will be different from his. I wonder how he would have told it. I'll never know for sure, but I think he'd say he had a rollicking time everyday schmoozing with the psychiatrists and attendants that patronized The Royal Gardens.

He'd probably say that if he'd become a lawyer or a professor of languages as he'd planned, it would have bored him out of his brain and that he'd never have the adventures he experienced being the proprietor of The Royal Gardens. Most of all, despite the ups and downs of the business and the demons that haunted him, he'd say he'd miss working side by side with Mom, whom he loved dearly, even though he had a strange way of showing it sometimes and depended on her to keep the business going.

I learned early on that Mom and Dad's relationship was anything but smooth. Mom actually walked out on Dad a couple of times. Once, when I was a baby and she could no longer abide his mercurial moods, tantrums, and demands, she bundled me up. We set out by train for Baltimore, her hometown, so she could gain perspective about how she wanted to live the rest of her life because the way it was playing out wasn't working for her.

The first time Mom left Dad, she hitchhiked to the train station in Philly to reach her family home in Maryland. Her mother Carmella, hounded by her sister-in-law, Aunt Lena, who had never married or had kids, pleaded with Mom every day to go back to The Royal Gardens, telling her how much Dad missed us. Although we were gone for a short time, that must have seemed like forever to him.

However, before long, Dad regressed into his old patterns of stinginess and criticism if everything wasn't exactly to his liking: his dinner, her clothes, and the way she interacted with the customers. Once he accused her of flirting with a man at the bar who had no teeth, horrible BO, and showed off his muscles by wearing sleeveless t-shirts.

If dinner wasn't on the table at the same time every night, he'd berate Mom. "What is wrong with you? I'm starved from working all day. My dinner should be ready before the next wave of customers shows up. Is that too much to ask?"

Mom walked out on Dad a second time, a couple of years after we'd moved to a suburban ranch house with three bedrooms, one bath (where everyone seemed to sequester every time I had to pee), and an acre of lush ground where Mom planted red roses and geraniums, and put up a clothesline where the sheets flapped around in the breeze every day the sun came out. One day, Dad and I bordered the pavement with purple and yellow pansies. It's one of the happiest days I spent with Dad. I still have a picture.

I was sixteen and a junior in high school with a brother seven years younger and a sister who was born when my parents were ancient by my standards. My sister was still a baby when Mom asked me to join her in the yard so she could tell me that she'd be leaving for the weekend. She spilled her sorrow as we stood by the clothesline, the sheets flapping against our faces in the breeze. She said she'd received an anonymous phone call from a rough-and tumble-sounding woman named Ada, who claimed she was having an affair with my father.

Mom made a couple of phone calls to verify what the woman told her and found it plausible that my dad was involved with this woman, who seemed, from the way Mom described her, to be the antithesis of Mom with her brassy tone, poor grammar, and cocky attitude.

Again, Mom decided to take off for Baltimore, her childhood home. My grandmother and Aunt Lena had died years before, so there was no one to stop Mom from leaving Dad and staying as long as she wanted. Her family embraced her and invited her to stay with them until she could decide what to do about Dad cheating on her.

Feeling guilty for leaving my brother and me to care for our baby sister, she arrived home after a weekend in a state of confusion, not knowing any more about what to do than when she left. I was so happy to see Mom back that I couldn't stop laughing and crying all day. I made her promise never to leave again no matter what, and she hugged me so tight she almost broke my bones, and said, "I promise." She kept that promise until her final day on earth.

My brother, a child himself, and I took turns caring for our sister in Mom's absence. I admit that I was not the best caregiver for a baby as I fumbled when changing her diapers and feeding her. I'd never enjoyed babysitting or any of my mom's other domestic talents even though I loved my sister dearly.

My father often blasted me out because of this shortcoming. According to him, the main reason women were on earth was to serve men and raise the kids. He couldn't stand that I had different ideas. When Mom left the second time, I was frying burgers on the stove when the skillet caught fire. My brother acted quickly and doused the fire with a pail of water.

"You can't do anything right," Dad shouted, surveying the damage and charred burgers. "How can you ever hope to be a good wife or mother like your mom.

"I'm going to go to college and get a great job so I don't have to be a maid like you expect Mom to be," I shouted back. He repeated that I was an abysmal failure and told me how I bungled everything I touched. Dad loved repeating things. He didn't talk to me the rest of the time Mom was away, and I was glad.

Back when we lived at the Royal Gardens, Mom often worked ten hours a day with no paycheck. If she needed money, she'd ask Dad for the exact amount she needed to pay bills, and he'd dole it out. If he thought her request was justified, he'd count the money out in Italian, slapping each bill on her hand with a dramatic flourish: "Uno, due, tre, quattro…"

If Dad didn't feel that Mom needed the money that day, she was forced to scrimp and scramble to make ends meet even though my parents reaped a modest profit from their business. Although many women in those days kowtowed to their husbands, even as a child, I always felt that their marriage was out of whack. Unlike most of the other kids' moms, she never had any mad money to spend on clothes or little luxuries she wanted, like movies, make-up, or lunch out with her lady friends.

Why should Mom get short-changed? Why did I have to hear her crying in her bedroom at night after Dad made her unhappy during the day? Dad always stayed at the bar until one in the morning and then went out barhopping to after-hours clubs after he shooed everyone out of his bar.

Because Dad had boundless energy, he was able to get by on very little sleep.

Mom often spent her evenings alone or with me, listening to scary radio shows, like "Inner Sanctum," "The Fat Man," and "The Creaking Door." Nightly, we turned on our radio and a monologue like this chilled me: "We bring you the tops in spine chillers (enter the sound of the creaking door)." I was so scared I almost peed myself. Mom laughed at the host's theatrics, but my eyes widened in fear.

Dad usually returned home to our apartment about three hours before the light peeked through my window. I saw the sadness in Mom's face as I heard his key in the door, but she and Dad just said "hi" when he came upstairs. We said good night, and I traipsed to my room to await the *whee woo* sound of the Royal Gardens sign and the dead reaching out to me from the Roosevelt cemetery to let me know everything would turn out all right no matter what.

Dad smiled and joked with his customers who loved him, but he could be a tyrant with Mom, ordering her around and telling her she didn't measure up. When they'd argue, I'd sometimes seek out Miss Laura and bury my head in her roomy apron. "Now, now, honey," she'd say. "They don't mean anything by it. All couples fight, but I know they love each other, and they'll stay together no matter what. So, no need to worry. And besides, Miss Laura is always here for you. You know that baby."

By seeing how my parents coped with one another's disparate personalities and dealt with their conflicts, I somehow learned that it's important to work through problems in a marriage, no matter how impossible they seem. I don't think they ever got to that point, but they loved each other in their own way, even though many observers might not see it as a healthy kind of love. I could tell it wasn't.

Chapter Two
Miss Clara, the Waitress Who Knew about God

Q. Why did God make you?"
A. God made me to know Him, to love Him, and to serve Him in this
world, and to be happy with Him forever in the next."
— Miss Clara teaching me Catechism

Over the next few months, Dad's volatile moods stabilized with drugs prescribed by his doctors. Once, they gave him shock treatments, which terrified him, so he insisted on going back to his daily regimen of drugs and talk therapy. He tried not to go the talk route too often, probably because he had the shrinks at the bar to give him their brand (with a few shots and beers to fortify them) of psychoanalysis.

Sometimes, he still gave mom a rough time if his dinner wasn't ready on time or if she paid what he perceived as too much attention to a grisly guy at the bar. He'd blast me and my brother out if we talked back to either of them, but that seemed within the realm of normal parental discipline.

However, once as a punishment for acting up at the bar, he took me upstairs to our apartment and pinched my butt repeatedly, which to me, appeared to be a form of medieval torture. I guess he thought the punishment fit the crime of being a mouthy kid, in his view, that warranted more than walloping my bottom. I reacted with blood-curdling screams to the pinching, which brought Mom racing up the steps to put a stop to this grotesque punishment. I wondered what the customers thought, but they'd witnessed my antics many times, so I guessed they thought I deserved whatever horrible fate befell me.

Dad and Mom started getting along better after he told her he'd never do anything to make her leave him again. He'd even surprise her with gifts of lacy lingerie or Lily of the Valley, her favorite perfume, to show her he intended to change. According to him, he never touched another woman, not ever, especially not the likes of icky Ada. Grace was the only one for him, and she eventually forgave him for cheating, but I could tell she never forgot. She always said, "You can forgive, but you can't forget."

Growing up in a taproom brought me in close contact with an interesting array of employees, family members, and patrons. Because of how hard our home was to get to because it was plopped in the middle of the Super Highway, few kids came to visit. Their parents didn't relish the idea of our apartment being that close to Byberry, the state mental hospital, and their kids coming into contact with people who drank as a sport. They also hated the drive because they felt that an erratic driver could plow into their car without provocation. At least, that's what they told Mom and Dad.

Miss Clara, the waitress, was a fixture at The Royal Gardens. Every afternoon, she'd don her white uniform and hair net like a queen preparing to hold court with her subjects, her regular patrons. Super-skinny, street-smart, and sporting a bleached blond page boy, she never let my dad, the restaurant customers, or the guys at the bar intimidate her. Like Miss Laura, Miss Clara always held the upper hand and wasn't afraid to let people know she ruled the roost. If you got on her nerves, she'd get right up in your face and blow billows of Camel cigarette smoke straight at your nostrils and chuckle wildly when you cringed.

She knew every item on the menu and could describe it to a tee. "Do you guys want your usual rare rump roast and cheese-stuffed spuds, or would you prefer shrimp with mushrooms over fettuccini?" she'd ask the customers, calling them by name. Miss Clara clarified all special customer requests for my mom, otherwise known as Grace, the cook. That way a customer never left the restaurant disappointed.

Carlo, a fussy customer, always ordered every shrimp dish (even Scampi) with no oil. It worked like a laxative on him, he told us in a whisper, craning his beefy neck our way to be sure no one heard. He thought talking about poop in public was unbefitting a gentleman of his stature as a high school math teacher at Central, one of the most prestigious public schools in Philly.

He also wanted to be sure garlic was left out of his favorite dishes so his lady friends would find him debonair and sexy when he made his move on them, which he did whenever he had the chance. Garlic would dampen the mood for them and him, and at his age, he needed everything he could muster to rev up his libido. Viagra wasn't on the market yet. Miss Clara started calling him "no oil, no garlic" straight to his face. When Clara placed the order, Mom immediately knew how to cook for him because she knew his hashtag before hashtags were invented.

Everyone who worked at The Royal Gardens had names for people. Dad called it "an Italian thing," but I heard people of all ethnicities and educational levels calling people weird names like "BO Plenty" (use your imagination) and Sucker Punch, after a guy who once punched a bartender after he'd gotten pissed because the bar tender flagged him before he got too drunk to drive back to Byberry Hospital where he worked in maintenance.

Clara and my parents had names for a lot of customers, especially the ones who worked at the hospital, like "Bug House John" (don't ask), and Vera a nurse, aka, "Miss Henny Penny" (she was afraid of everyone who looked suspicious to her, like Mo, an attendant who masked his face with a long gray beard (he must have been butt ugly beneath those whiskers), or someone who asked uncomfortable questions, like Dr. Palinski, the head psychiatrist at Byberry, "How the hell old are you, Vera? You've been coming here since before I was born. To which she replied, "Why do you want to know that (a la Dear Abby) or "None of your beeswax, Doc."

Miss Clara and Mom named Jennifer, one of the restaurant regulars' kids, "Baked Potato" because she asked her mom to cut up the baked potato, she always ordered with her chicken fingers kids' platter. An only child, her mom and dad kept her young beyond her years and unable to do anything for herself, except to use the bathroom.

One day Clara could no longer abide seeing a perfectly capable pre-teen acting whiny and helpless and she blurted out, "Try cutting it up yourself, Jennifer. You're a big girl now. Your parents and Miss Clara need you to grow up."

Jennifer shoved her food away and burst out crying, and her parents didn't appear at the restaurant for a while. When my mom and dad wondered why they hadn't seen "baked potato" and her parents, Clara shrugged it off and said, "Maybe they got sick of cutting her baked potatoes and huffing and puffing on her dinner so it wouldn't burn her precious little lips." Naturally, the family couldn't stay away and returned in two weeks. This time Jennifer ordered French fries instead of a baked potato rather than face Miss Clara's wrath.

"Mr. Clean," a hefty guy with a zillion tattoos, bushy white eyebrows, and a shaved head clean as a baby's butt, was Mr. Fixit for the business. He was a dead ringer for the guy in the cleaning fluid commercial back in the day. If the stove or walk-in freezer was on the blink, Mr. Clean appeared pronto to fix it and handed my dad a hefty bill. He could change lightbulbs that were too high up for dad to tackle or plunge and snake a murky toilet that the barflies filled with loose feces from downing too many draft beers and bowls of peanuts. He appeared like a genie when you called him to fix, plunge, clean, and paint. When he left, he'd repeat the TV slogan, "There's no clean like Mr. Clean," and would hand Dad his inflated bill.

"The Exterminator" was simply that. He'd come on a monthly basis to purge the place of rats, mice, and creepy bugs that hopped and buzzed, especially in the kitchen and bathroom. Being a perpetually curious child, I asked the exterminator to describe the worst thing he met up with in his business. He shuddered and told me that one Friday he got a desperate call from Raymond, an elderly homeowner in Philly, about mouse infestation in his row house.

Raymond implored him to come quickly, so the exterminator, devoted to his job, showed up as fast as he could catch the subway into town. When the exterminator arrived at the home overrun with weeds and porch clutter, an elderly man with long curly hair greeted him with bumps and lumps jutting out of his head like snakes. He held out his hand, but the exterminator waved it away.

"Hey, I'm Raymond. Thanks for coming," he said, tugging at his hair.

The exterminator wasn't prepared for what he saw. It turns out that a pair of mice had taken up residence in Raymond's hair, entangling themselves in his unruly white locks. The exterminator shouted, "Are you kidding me, man?" His voice wafted throughout the complex, prompting the neighbors to open their shades to get a peek.

They'd known for years that the old man was strange and stayed away from him, but the exterminator's shouts drove them outside with their cameras to immortalize the moment for their families. Shortly after, a reporter for a national scandal sheet caught wind of it and interviewed some of Raymond's neighbors for his tabloid. The man with the mouse hair threatened to sue, so the paper backed off and left without printing his story.

Once the exterminator regained his composure, he asked Raymond why he let things get so out-of-control. He said that at first, he thought the mice were cute, and he decided to keep them as pets, but then they took over the house and he couldn't escape their clutches. They ate and slept with him, crawled all over him, and made his hair home.

What could the exterminator do to help him escape this mess, or was he doomed? First, the exterminator grabbed a spray bottle with, of all things, Mr. Clean, and directed the powerful elixir to the man's head. The mice ran to any holes in the wall they could find. Then the exterminator sprayed poison in every nook and cranny in the mouse-overrun house. He told Raymond to call him after he'd disposed of the mouse corpses and droppings and hurriedly left. The exterminator later learned that the neighbors told the cops about hearing the exterminator scream when he saw the mice, and those lucky enough to have the latest technology showed them the photos they'd taken on their Polaroid cameras. The city quickly evicted Raymond and condemned the house.

Making up names for people may seem childish and silly, but some people in my family still do it, finding a way to vent on annoying people. It may seem uncharitable, but it affords them satisfaction, and, in some instances, revenge, for dealing with impossible people when nothing else works.

Besides playing the name game with my parents, Miss Clara was my religion teacher for my Catholic School Catechism classes from first through fifth grade. Every night before the dinner crowd descended on the restaurant, Miss Clara and I sat at an empty table, nibbling cheddar cheese and crackers. She downed at least three cups of black coffee to keep her awake for her dinner shift, while I drank whatever soda I wanted from the bar, mainly cherry cola on the rocks with two cherries.

Dad replenished our drinks and checked in to see how well I was learning the tenets of my religion from Miss Clara, the waitress. Dad didn't care that she was a non-denominational Protestant and rarely attended

Church, as long as she was willing to indoctrinate me so that when I died I'd go straight to heaven as a faithful follower of the Catholic faith and bypass the flames of Purgatory, or, God forbid, Hell.

During our Catechism sessions, Clara asked, and I answered each question like a robot. Sometimes I understood what I was saying, but other answers were vague and mysterious. Here are some easy ones that I didn't have to think to answer.

Q: Who made you?

A. God made me.

Q. Who are you?

A. I am a child of God

Q. Who is God?

A. God is the Creator of heaven and earth, and of all things.

Miss Clara would usually glare at me and tell me to memorize the answers. It didn't matter if I didn't understand. Who the heck cared as long as you could parrot them back? Understanding them would come when you got older. Even *she* didn't understand the questions and answers, and she attended Rock of Ages Bible School for twelve years with Pastor Jim, an authority on salvation.

Here are a couple of the harder ones that I asked Clara to explain:

Q. What is mortal sin?

A. Mortal sin is a grievous offense against the law of God.

I asked Miss Clara how bad a sin had to be to be considered mortal. Some priests said that eating meat on Friday was mortal, but others said that God wouldn't damn us to hell for something as trivial as that.

Q. What is venial sin?

A. Venial sin is a slight offense against the law of God in matters of less importance; or, in matters of great importance, it is an offence committed without sufficient reflection or full consent of the will.

Venial sin was another story. I took it to mean giving the food you hated, like liver and onions or lima beans, to the dog, who was hiding under the table licking his chops. I didn't know what the second part of the answer meant when it mentioned "sufficient reflection." Did that mean I'd committed the sin without thinking hard enough about whether it was a sin, and that I wouldn't be held guilty because I did it without mulling it over in my brain? Who knew?

The second part of the answer baffled me as much as it did Miss Clara as she lit up another cigarette and fumbled for an answer. It's hard to tell if you gave full consent. Maybe the dog's tongue was hanging out because he was hungry, and maybe you hated liver and lima beans, so you said to yourself, "Oh who cares, and shoved the food into your pet's salivating mouth without thinking about full consent of your will, whatever that is.

Q. Why did God make you?"

A. God made me to know Him, to love Him, and to serve Him in this world, and to be happy with Him forever in the next.

I really liked this one. God sounded like a lovable spirit. However, I sometimes wondered if there was really a next world (I hoped there was so I wouldn't rot in a grave or a mausoleum like my friends who talked to me in the Roosevelt Cemetery), or if those priests who wrote the Catechism told us stuff like that to keep us in line while we were on this earth so we'd give our money to the collection box every Sunday.

Religion could give you anxiety attacks sometimes. It actually made me want to talk to the psychiatrists at the bar about my doubts and questions. But here I was with Miss Clara learning the Catechism, and I had to answer the questions without getting her nervous or she'd make me sit down for another session after the customers ate dinner. By that time, she'd be her worst chain-smoking self after putting up with "baked potato" and "no oil, no garlic."

In retrospect, I'm glad I learned the Catechism from Miss Clara. She taught me that you don't have to believe in something to teach it. You have to be a good salesperson and try to explain the facts you want the person to learn in the best possible way. Maybe I became a teacher because I had so many good ones, like Miss Clara.

Clara also liked it when I asked her the hard questions. Even though she didn't answer them for fear of getting on the bad side of my parents, she said that it's good to question everything and to draw your own conclusions. After all, that's one reason she stopped going to the non-denominational church, plus the fact she didn't like anyone telling her what to do.

While Miss Clara worked at the restaurant, we found out that her teenaged daughter Eva suffered from anorexia, an eating disorder. Miss Clara tried everything to help her, but she ended up dying from the disease. I saw her once when her mother bought her in the restaurant. Her bones stuck out of her body, and she looked pale and weak. I often wonder if that had any influence on Miss Clara's religious beliefs. I never talked with her about her daughter as I couldn't believe such a terrible thing should happen to a young girl not that much older than me. Most of all, I hated to see Miss Clara cry as she sometimes did when she mentioned Eva and her illness. I loved her like an aunt.

Even back then, I questioned all the institutions that served me. To this day, I wonder why the Catholic Church condemns "artificial" birth control. Would God, being who He is with so many important things to worry about, really give a hoot whether every sperm unites with every egg? And even if he did, would he damn you to hell's flames forever if you used contraception?

Would He care if you spent time thinking about mortal and venial sins and deciding which was which? Wouldn't God cut you some slack and understand if you didn't know what "sufficient reflection" and "full consent" meant in His infallible mind?

I could also never understand the church's condemnation of divorce. Suppose you both hated one another's guts and your life was hell, or if one or both parties abused the other physically or emotionally? Wouldn't you be better off divorcing? These and other questions came to mind as I began to think more about what it meant to be a free-thinking woman who grew up in a bar with Miss Clara as my first religion teacher.

That said, I love a lot about Catholicism: the concept of an all-loving God who is always willing to forgive you, no matter how despicably you act; the presence and intervention of angels and saints in our lives; and the meaningful rituals at all stages of life, from birth to death. I still don't like the sexism, the focus on sex, the rigidity of it all, and the possibility of hell, but, hey, that's just me. Whatever you decide about religion is right for you.

Chapter Three
Uncle Tony and the Cabins

"Can you mark this test for me now, Catty School? I can't wait to see what I got."
—*Uncle Tony*

Dad's mental outlook seemed to stabilize more because of medicine and talk therapy, but we knew his emotional problems were always there, so Mom stayed on guard for fear he'd regress. Aside from occasional rants about his dinner not reaching the table on time (5:00 PM),. or a few choice curse words about my zooming around the bar pestering the psychiatrists and occasional Byberry patients sneaking in, Dad presented himself as "Joe the Bartender," beloved by all.

Nobody knew the full extent of his illness, not even Miss Laura or Clara, the waitress. They saw his sudden mood changes, bouts of irritability, and shifts from mania to sadness, but they never knew how serious his problems were and, if they did, they never asked. Even when Mom took off to seek refuge with her mother and siblings in Baltimore, Mom told me they figured it was a well-needed vacation from the stresses of work. They all knew that things weren't cool with her and Dad, but they didn't grasp the gravity of it.

The main thing that changed at the Royal Gardens that year was the increased traffic around the building's periphery. My grandparents built a few small cabins in back of the bar to generate more income for our families. The cabins turned out to be a profitable venture since there weren't many places to rent along the Superhighway if you were looking for a place to shack up in the middle of the afternoon in the middle of nowhere. Of course, there was the added benefit of a tasty meal, like chicken marsala, or pot roast, whipped up by my mom, Grace. But few of these cabin renters wanted to take a chance blowing their covers, so they'd buy cold cuts and soda at the small deli down the road to tide them over until they returned home to their husbands and wives, who didn't know about their wild escapades.

As a six-year-old, I couldn't grasp the hoopla around Uncle Tony's cabins so I questioned Mom one day when people waited in line to have my uncle escort them to a cabin where they'd make whoopie to their hearts' content, without worrying someone would find out. Of course, the dead souls in The Roosevelt Cemetery across the street would never tell because they didn't talk to anyone but me, as far as I knew.

"Mom," I asked, pointing to the cabins "why are those people sleeping in the afternoon"?

Mom, never one to discuss what she called "the birds and the bees" smiled. "I guess they need a break from driving. When Uncle Tony's not busy, go keep him company," she said, changing the subject, like she always did when things got awkward.

I wandered off to the main cabin where Uncle Tony, Dad's older brother, collected the money and ushered guests to their cozy cabin, where they'd stay for a few hours, hump to their hearts' content, and return home, like their cabin trysts had never happened. I'd overheard Miss Laura talking about the adventures of the cabin dwellers, and, at the time, wondered what it all meant. I thought *hump* might have been some kind of wild dance like the jitterbug or calypso. If it was, why would they try to hide it from their families?

The master cabin provided a full bath, a kitchenette, and sleeping quarters for my Uncle Tony, who became the cabin manager, a step up from the farm hand position he held from the time he was in sixth grade when my grandparents took him out of school. Although compulsory education was the rule, somehow my grandparents got around it.

Rotund and balding, Uncle Tony was his parents' workhorse on their farm, and now they put him in charge of the cabins, a step up for him, and a job he proudly carried out. Some family members proclaimed Tony autistic because of his behavior patterns. For one thing, he showed limited eye contact. He also repeated himself when he spoke, along with repeating certain behaviors, like using unusual words he made up and hand gestures to accompany them.

Even then, people thought he had mental health issues, maybe anxiety and OCD, but people didn't talk about those things that much in the olden days. He thought of himself as perfectly normal and functioned well despite his unusual ways.

Others proclaimed him socially challenged because he never interacted with other people in our neighborhood. People could say what they wanted about Uncle Tony, but I knew that a few years after he retired from running the cabins, he singlehandedly ministered to Aunt Minnie, his sister, during her final memory-related illness.

Tony called me "Catty School" because I always had a book in my hand. One spring day he called my mom and asked if Catty School could come out to the main cabin to visit. Mom and Dad frequently sent me there to deliver food or he would have subsisted on fig newtons and chocolate milk.

That day he said he had a surprise for me. Mom sent me to the cabin with a paper bag filled with her famous pepper and egg sandwiches on Italian bread that made the "'Merigans" (Americans) at the bar salivate. Dad threw in a can of Budweiser and a bag of salted peanuts.

When I got to the cabin, Uncle Tony was looking over the math test I'd given him the day before. I dropped the soggy sandwiches, beer, and peanuts on his desk and popped the beer can so he could drink out of it. You'd think I'd given him a winning lottery ticket; he was so ecstatic. He gummed the sandwich and chug-a-lugged the beer.

"Hey, Uncle Tony, I heard you wanted to see me," I said after I polished off the nuts he shared.

He lumbered over to the metal cabinet where he kept his surprises for family members. He handed me a milk chocolate bunny in a white chocolate Easter basket, a surprise he must have saved up for months from his meager salary as concierge-in-chief of the cabins. The cabin visitors loved him dearly and often gifted him with dollar bills for making them feel at home. He left little bags of Fig Newtons, his favorite snack, on their bedside tables and turned down the covers so guests would feel like they were at a 4-star hotel.

After basking in my approval for the candy, Uncle Tony pulled a math test out of the drawer and said, "Can you mark this test for me now, Catty school? I can't wait to see what I got."

I scanned the test, took out my red pen and marked 100% A+ at the top.

"Yippee-kay-yay," he shouted, and danced around waving his hands like he always did when he scored well in a test, which was nearly every time. He told me that's how cowboys used to talk, and he loved pretending he was a cowboy. Uncle Tony sometimes made up his own weird words, and I wondered if all adults acted like him when no one else was around. One day after we worked on times tables with flash cards, he told me about a strange word he made up and used often—*Relsteen.* He said you must always capitalize it because it was a magical word that could bring you happiness whenever you used it.

Uncle Tony said that one day when he was twelve and Dad was ten, they decided to take a walk in the woods back of the farm. When it started drizzling, they never thought it would turn into a major storm, so they kept walking. As Uncle Tony tells it, they started shouting for the rain to stop. They couldn't see where they were going in the blinding downpour and feared that lightning would strike. They'd already seen a few sparks zigzagging across the darkening sky. Thunder boomed in unrelenting fury as the rain pelted their soaked bodies.

Tony thumped my dad on the back. Dad frowned. "Yo, Brother, you know how I hate it when you punch me. You're stronger than you think."

Uncle Tony laughed. According to Dad, they were both scared shitless, but Tony always laughed no matter how bad things got. He'd never admit to being afraid of anything.

"Listen, Joe Bones," he told Dad, "I'm going to get us out of this mess." He gave Dad a fist bump before anyone had heard of one. It nearly knocked over my scrawny father, lovingly dubbed "Joe Bones" by his friends at Bensalem High School.

Uncle Tony lowered his voice even though Dad was the only one around. He couldn't stand taking the chance of anyone making fun of him, although he intimidated the kids in the neighborhood with his gargantuan size and unusual ways.

"Here's what we're going to do, Joe Bones. I know a magic word that always works."

Dad laughed. "You're saying it's going to stop the storm, Tony? Your magic word will stop the storm and we'll be safe?"

Uncle Tony punched Dad's shoulder again, this time a little harder. "Laugh all you want," Then he shouted out the word *Relsteen* and spelled it for Dad. R-E-L-S-T-E-E-N. And remember it always has a capital R."

Dad scoffed. "What the hell, Tony?"

Uncle Tony ignored him and began to add a rain dance to his magic word. He grabbed Dad's hands and danced him around in a circle in the middle of the woods until he and Dad became two dervishes, whirling in total synchrony. Uncle Tony told me how the tree branches belted them, and bird poop smacked their cheeks and made them white. Uncle Tony was shouting now: "Repeat after me: 'Relsteen, Relsteen, Relsteen.'"

Dad went along with it, but he couldn't stop laughing. The two brothers danced until Dad yelled, "Enough, Tony. I'm going to poop my pants if you don't stop."

"Look, Joe Bones, Look," Tony said, bringing the dance to a sudden halt. He pointed to the sky. "I told you the rain would stop."

Dad stared at the sky in amazement. "Damn, and it did, Brother," he said, and they both raced each other back to the farm.

To Dad's surprise and according to Uncle Tony's prediction, the rain stopped. Was it a coincidence, or did my uncle make it happen with his magic word? They would never know, but Dad swore by the ritual until he tried it himself when another storm struck. Much to his chagrin, he began to believe that Uncle Tony alone had the magic touch.

Uncle Tony began to use his magic word whenever he wanted something to happen or for no reason at all. He viewed it as a catchall word as Philadelphians often use the word *jawn* today. *Relsteen* could mean anything. It could mean how to fix a major problem by creating a rain dance when you're stuck in the middle of a storm in a forest, saying everything's going to turn out fine when you have serious doubts, or telling a person who harasses you to bug off.

Uncle Tony loved his magic word, but one day Father O'Loughlin, his parish priest, told the people at Mass that believing in magic or supernatural solutions to problems was against the Catholic faith. Tony became fearful that he'd burn in hell if he continued saying the magic word. The priest heard that some of the locals had visited a psychic at a neighborhood fair and wanted to set them straight before they'd commit a mortal sin and put their immortal souls in jeopardy.

Years after the rain dance episode, Uncle Tony had lived with a guilty conscience long enough. He decided this was time to confess what he perceived as his worst sin to Father O'Loughlin, the priest at St. Matt's. He closed the confessional door and waited for the priest to slide the little trap door that allowed him to hear his penitent. "Tell me your sins, my child," Father said, heaving a sigh. He'd peeked and saw that it was Uncle Tony. Again.

"Father, I did Relsteen," Tony said in a whisper, ashamed to confess his deepest, darkest sin.

"You did *what*, Anthony, I mean my son?" Father boomed in a stage whisper, causing the people waiting outside the confessional to wonder what kind of sin this man confessed for Father to respond so angrily. They'd always thought of the priest as mild-mannered.

Uncle Tony repeated his transgression, this time shouting it out. "Relsteen, Father. It's a repetitive action (Tony could use big words when he felt like it.) "It's like when you're stuck in the middle of a bad situation and you say it to make things better, and you keep saying it because it works."

According to Tony, Father O'Loughlin closed his eyes and said, "Stop the foolishness, now, Anthony. The word is ridiculous, and you're ridiculous thinking it's a sin to say it. Stop doing it."

"But you said at Mass that magic words were bad. I never forgot that, Father."

"I'm telling you now to forget it, Anthony. It wasn't meant to be taken literally."

"Say what, Father?"

The priest exhaled loudly. "Your sins are forgiven, Anthony. Go in peace. For your penance, say two rosaries, and if that's not enough to assuage your guilt, add five *Our Fathers*."

Uncle Tony told me he vowed never to say *Relsteen* again. After all, saying two rosaries was more than he could bear. Forget the Our Fathers.

Years later, Anthony, as Father O'Loughlon called him, went back on his word about not saying *Relsteen*. One day when my brother Joe tried to visit him in his little cubby in the basement in my grandparents' farmhouse, he thought it was the only thing that could get Joe to go back home. Joe had driven all the way from Bucks County to Philly (a forty-minute drive) to visit my elderly Aunt Minnie and Uncle Tony. Caps for Aunt Minnie.

When he arrived at their rowhouse, Aunt Minnie did her best to coax Uncle Tony out of the small bathroom in his basement cubby. Uncle Tony heard my brother's voice, and he shouted, "I'm taking a crap." Tony was great at making up excuses, even when they were tall tales, which they usually were. I was there when all this happened and couldn't stop laughing, even though I felt sorry for Uncle Tony and my brother.

Uncle Tony was hellbent on locking himself in the bathroom to avoid seeing Joe. He'd open the door ever so slightly and close it again until he felt satisfied that Joe had taken the Boulevard back to Bucks County. Joe could hear our uncle mumbling *Relsteen* with the distinct purpose of getting him to exit the premises. After all, Uncle Tony reasoned, it was a magic word and gave him supernatural powers when he was caught in a storm. Who was to say it wouldn't work now with his nephew pounding on his bathroom door?

After Joe left without seeing Uncle Tony, Aunt Minnie told me that her brother didn't want to see Joe because he had a Golden Retriever and that dogs frightened him more than being damned to hell because of saying *Relsteen*. If he talked to Joe, the dog might hunt him down and attack him. When Joe went to see Tony in his cabin a few years after that, Tony showed Joe one of those white fuzzy balls, called pappi, that you blow on to scatter dandelion seeds. "If you blow on this dandelion real hard, a big hurricane will come," Tony said.

Joe, of course, laughed it off. The next week, we got clobbered by Hurricane Hazel. After that, we all wondered if Tony definitely had magical powers.

One day when Uncle Tony was in his nineties and refused to go to the hospital for what appeared to be a serious illness, a relative, who checked in on him since Aunt Minnie had died, found him slumped over his desk in his basement cubby. She called an ambulance, but Tony refused treatment. He died a short time later. When family members cleaned out his desk, they found tests I'd marked, all his school papers, and a half-full box of Fig Newtons.

The family asked Father O'Loughlin to give his eulogy, and he graciously obliged. He began it this way: "Anthony was a plain and simple man who took care of his sister Philomena (Aunt Minnie) during her final fight with Dementia. He walked to the corner store and prepared grilled cheese and tomato sandwiches for her. He was always there for her even though he was ailing himself with his own health problems and the demons that haunted him.

"Anthony,' "Father O'Loughlin said, like my uncle had appeared in front of him wearing his overalls, red suspenders and Phillies cap, "We will always cherish your innocence when the rest of the world is jaded and skeptical. Remember that it was Jesus who said, "Truly I say unto you, unless you become like children, you will never enter the kingdom of heaven."

Father looked at the congregation. "I'll stop singing Anthony's praises now. I think that's the way he would have wanted it. One thing he hated was long, boring sermons and phony accolades. When I went on too long with my sermons, he'd say, 'Can you make it shorter next time, Father? In ten minutes. I'll start to doze off. No offense.'" The audience laughed.

That rainy Tuesday, family, friends, and neighbors from the rowhouses in northeast Philly where my grandparents had lived out their final years, came out to honor Uncle Tony, a simple man who understood that life's true meaning was to love and help one another. Just as Father ended his eulogy, the sun peeped through. Uncle Tony's magic word, *relsteen,* must have kicked in one last time. I wondered if Father O'Loughlin thought so too.

I learned from Uncle Tony that you can't buy kindness and compassion, that it comes naturally if you're seeking it. I also learned that you don't need a college degree to have common sense and good intentions. After all, Dad had a college degree, and it didn't help him deal with his emotional issues. Street smarts go a long way toward living a productive and authentic life, the best life any of us can hope to live. What do you think?

Uncle Tony taught me that even if people perceive you as different, strange, or apart from the mainstream or what people deem "normal," it's what you think of yourself that's important. The hell with everybody else because it doesn't matter in the end.

Chapter Four
Dr. Palinski and the Yummy Fries

"Grace, make me another basket of your yummy fries."
—Dr. Alex Palinski

From five to seven p.m. every day, Dr. Alexi Palinski, AKA Doctor Alex, showed up at Dad's bar after making psychiatric rounds at Byberry Hospital. Dad drew one beer and then another for Doc until he let out a loud burp and somebody at the bar would say, "I think you've had enough, Doc." The guys at the bar made fun of Doc because three beers were his limit. He weighed about four hundred pounds but couldn't drink like the other guys.

Doc said he didn't drink much because he had to keep his brain sharp to help his patients, but the truth was he couldn't handle it. He was assigned some of the most violent patients at Byberry Hospital, but for some reason, they didn't threaten him like they did the other doctors and the hospital attendants, the workers who dealt with the patients first-hand.

One of the attendants, James Cuff, told us how Doc pried a patient they nicknamed "Wolfman" off James' back by resting his beefy hand on the guy's shoulder, rubbing his arm, and singing "Three Coins in a Fountain " a la Frank Sinatra, like he was Wolfman's mama. Doc had a knack with patients, but he had trouble controlling his own son, Champ.

"Take your meds," Dr. Alex told Wolfman. "It's not a big deal, and you'll feel better. Mr. Cuff is here to help when you're ready."

"Okay, Doc, but I want you, not Cuff, to give them to me."

"At your service," Doc said with a little bow, and Wolfman complied.

Doc's favorite meal at the Royal Gardens at the bar or straddling a folding chair in Mom's kitchen was a huge basket of Mom's French Fries deep fried in lard, blanched, and cooked crispy. No one made fries like Mom, not even Cliff, who became famous for his "Cliff's Home of the French-Fried Hot Dog" down the road. Years later, Cliff gave me my first job as a waitress. I loved the hot dogs, but it turned me off when Cliff sweat into my platter. He always gave me two hot dogs and a double helping of fries. That made up for it.

After Doc Alex polished off two baskets of fries, he'd run his tongue over his blubbery lips and say, "Grace, make me another basket of your yummy fries.

"Coming up, Doc," Mom said with a smile, "but too many fries could be bad for you."

"Hell, Gracie. You sound like my wife, Thelma. Please indulge me this one time and give me more fries. I need them. Thelma's always on my back about packing on the pounds. Don't you start too. The Royal Gardens is the only place I can come to get peace."

Mom laughed and shook her head. "Coming up, Doc. You're a master of persuasion."

Doc winked. "That's why they call me the savvy shrink, Gracie."

When Doc was in the middle of devouring his second basket of fries, like clockwork, as he did every day, Miss Thelma, his super-thin red-headed wife called, asking to talk to him. I hated answering the phone when Miss Thelma called.

"Come on, little one, I know he's there, so don't give me any bull-crap," she said in her usual crochety voice.

Doc put his finger up to his lips. "Tell her I just left," he whispered from across the room. He said that whenever she called. Miss Thelma always knew how to ask for what she wanted, and if she didn't get it— watch out.

I put my hand over the phone. I was starting to tear up. "I can't lie anymore, Doc. I don't want to go to hell. Miss Clara and I read about it in the Baltimore Catechism. Satan is the father of lies. It says so in the Bible. Lying is a mortal sin, and you can't expect me to do it. I *have* to tell Miss Thelma you're here."

Doc nearly choked on his fries and looked like he would fall from his chair, which would be a disaster since he was huge as a truck. He gave me a menacing look.

Mom rested her hands on her hips and stopped making orders. I could tell she was waiting to see what I would say to Doc's wife. She always encouraged me to think for myself.

I took my hand away from the phone. "He'll be home in a few minutes Mrs. Palinski," I said in my sweetest voice. "He's leaving now."

But Doc's wife wasn't having any of it. "Put that son-of-a-bitch on the phone now, little girl," she said in a voice that made her sound like the devil's bride.

Doc started gorging on the rest of the fries and washed them down with his beer. He shimmied out of his chair, wiped the ketchup off his mouth, and grabbed the phone from my hand. You could always tell what Doc was eating because it landed on his pants and his face.

Doc cleared his throat and made his voice gentle and sweet, like he was calming down one of his patients. "I'm on my way, Thelma. You told me you would make your Chicken Marsala tonight. I love how you baste it with that sweet white wine and sprinkle it with fresh rosemary. Are we still on for that? I wouldn't miss it for the world, sweetheart." Doc was a brown-noser at heart, especially when it came to Miss Thelma, but she never fell for it.

Doc didn't talk for a long time, so I wondered what was going on. I could hear Miss Thelma's raspy voice pouring out of the receiver. At one point, Doc moved the phone away from his ear. His hands shook and sweat beaded his forehead. I was dying to know what they were talking about. I tried not to be too obvious, but I wanted to know what was happening to make Doc so upset. We all cared about him and didn't want anything terrible to happen to him or his wife even though we all thought she was a whackadoodle.

"Did they arrest him?" Doc asked his wife. "Tell me it isn't true."

I could hear Doc's wife shouting in the background, and I picked up a few words like *school police* and *expulsion*. It didn't sound good. Before I could catch more of their conversation, Mom told me to go upstairs and start my homework. She knew I wouldn't be happy until I knew the whole story.

I went up to my room and took out my Dick and Jane reader. "Run, Spot, Run, run, run. Oh, oh, oh. Funny, funny Spot."

Oh heck, the stuff they gave us to read in school bored me out of my mind, so I took out a Nancy Drew book, *The Secret of the Old Clock*. Mom read to me from it every night, and soon I learned to read the books myself. I liked these books more than Dick and Jane and their dumb dog and cat, Spot and Puff. Why did we have to learn such useless stuff in school? If I ever became a teacher, I would never teach dumb stuff that people couldn't use in their everyday lives.

When I got back downstairs, Mom was hovering over Doc. She'd cleared Doc's empty fry basket and beer glass. Doc dropped his face in his hands. Mom went to the bar and told Dad to come to the kitchen. Dad asked Mr. Cuff, one of the regulars, to watch the bar for a while. "I'll give you a free refill when I get back," Dad said, and patted him on the shoulder.

Mr. Cuff was an attendant at Byberry, who came in every day after work with Doc Alex. Attendants had to do all the dirty work, stuff the doctors didn't do, like calm down patients and give out medicines. He usually wore a bright green corduroy shirt and khakis. He must have had about five pairs of each and wore clunky sneakers that squeaked when he walked. I heard he wasn't mean to the patients like some of the other attendants at the mental hospital.

"Sure thing, boss," Cuff said. Everyone called him Cuff, but since I was a kid, Dad said he was "Mr. Cuff" to me. Dad came into the kitchen to find Doc pacing the floor, his bushy salt and pepper hair flying all over like Albert Einstein. Ketchup spotted his seersucker suit that he bought in every color from Sears and Roebuck. He yanked off his tie and stuffed it in his pocket. "Damn tie's too tight. It's choking me," he said, but I figured he was talking about his life more than the tie.

Despite Dad's temper and changing moods, I could see in retrospect he had empathy, at least for certain people, although often not for close family members like me and Mom. He could put himself in someone's place and actually become that person. That's probably why his customers confided in him. He truly listened to people and gave the best advice. He helped them solve their own problems rather than giving them the answers they wanted to hear.

"I can see how upset you are, Doc." Dad said, resting his arm on Doc's.

"As you know, Joe, Champ is our only child, and we had high hopes for him. We groomed him to become a doctor like me, or a lawyer, but he dashed his chances for success."

"If it's any consolation, Doc. I went to law school and ended up being Joe, The Bartender, but that's not such a terrible thing. I get to talk to smart guys like you. I wouldn't trade my life for musty law books and demanding clients. Isn't that right, Grace?"

Mom rolled her eyes Maybe she was thinking how if Dad had become a lawyer, she wouldn't be stuck in the kitchen making fries for Doc or cooking big banquets for the Kiwanis Club.

"If Champ gets expelled," Doc said, "he'll have to transfer to public high school, and you can imagine what kind of trouble he'd get into there with no one to supervise him as they do in private school. After talking to Thelma today, I believe there's not much hope he'll change."

"What did Champ do this time, Doc?" Dad asked.

"Big trouble, Joe. The Dean suspended him for bringing liquor onto the campus."

I'd heard about Champ, Doc's sixteen-year-old son, who was a pain in the butt from the time he was a toddler. Things got worse when he started school. When he attended a fancy elementary school for rich kids, they asked him to leave because he tormented younger kids and started fights with classmates. Luckily, Doc knew a politician who was able to pull strings to get him into Mary Immaculate, a Catholic academy.

Nothing Doc and his wife tried helped with Champ. "When Champ was in eighth grade, we were out of town visiting my mother in her Philly apartment," Doc said. "Police raided our home for underage drinking, and the judge gave Champ a mild sentence: he'd have to clean the convent where his teachers lived. We grounded him for two months, but Champ didn't care."

Mom poured Doc a glass of iced tea to wash down the fries. "What else did Thelma tell you?" Mom asked.

"The Dean told Thelma that since this was his third offense (one for cheating, one for unruly conduct, and this one for underage drinking) they'd hold an expulsion hearing today to decide Champ's fate.

Doc glanced at his watch and struggled out of his chair. "Better get going. We have that meeting with the Dean and Champ at the school in an hour."

Mom packed a plastic container of pasta and meatballs so Doc and his wife wouldn't have to worry about dinner after their meeting. Dad turned to Doc on his way back to the bar. "Call if you need anything, Doc. We're here for you."

Doc raced out to his car to pick up Thelma so they could try to bail out Champ. Dad, Mom, and I watched him shimmy into his new Caddie luxury sedan and speed toward his house to pick up Miss Thelma. How I wanted to be a fly on the wall when they went to see the Dean.

After Doc left, Mom and Dad were cleaning up after the afternoon bar hoppers, and the night crowd got ready to take their place. "Do you want to hear what I think?" I asked, dancing around to "Hound Dog" blaring from the jukebox. I always told them what I thought even if they didn't want to know.

Mom smiled. "Do we have a choice?"

"Champ should get a job," I said. "it would help him grow up."

"Who would hire him with his lousy record?" Dad asked.

"*You* could," I said. Mom and Dad's eyes widened.

"Champ would work here?" Dad said.

"That's what I think would help him," I said.

The next day Doc showed up at the bar. "So how did it go at Champ's school with the Dean, Doc?" Dad asked. "Let's go into the kitchen where we can talk."

I put down my Nancy Drew book so I could hear what they said about Champ. Eavesdropping on adult conversations was my favorite thing.

Doc got right into it. "After a lot of apologies from us and bull-throwing on Champ's part, the Dean said, 'If Champ does one more thing, we'll expel him.'

The Dean said they've done everything they can for him. I know we've done all we could. Thelma and I sent him to counseling and bribed him by offering to buy him a car, but nothing worked."

Dad frowned. "Doc, you of all people should know that bribery never works."

Mom handed Doc a cola. "You give Champ too much already, Doc. That's part of the problem."

"Catherine has an idea, Doc," Dad said. "I wish I could take credit for it, but she thought of it on her own. I think sometimes kids know more than adults. She thinks he should get a part-time job."

Doc sighed." I'm all ears, but who would hire him if they found out about his problems?"

"We would," Dad, Mom, and I said at the same time.

Dad looked like he was going to cry. "You'd do that for me? What would he do if he worked here? He's never held a job in his life."

"He could help Miss Laura mop the floors," Dad said. "She's getting up in years, and it's getting harder for her these days. He could also be a dishwasher for the lunch crowd."

"I don't know how that would work out," Doc said.

"How so?" Mom asked.

"We've handed him a hefty allowance since he started high school. He'd rebel if we took it away."

Mom had made Doc a turkey and cheese on rye. She and Dad were worried that his diet of fries and beer would make his weight soar. He told them he now weighed 405 pounds, a five-pound increase from last month. I knew, even though I was only a kid, that you couldn't eat like that without the risk of a heart attack. We all worried about Doc's crazy eating habits. Mom gave him a few fries to keep him from complaining.

"It wouldn't hurt to talk to him about a part-time job.," Mom said. You could still give him a small allowance and tell him if he works here, he'll end up with more money than he had with only the allowance."

"I don't think he'll go for it," Doc said, shaking his head. "We've indulged Champ all his life, and now he doesn't know how to do anything for himself. "

"I don't think it will hurt to talk to him about it. I think he'd like the idea of making more money," I said. Back in the day, people would say I was a fresh kid, trying to weasel in on adult conversations, but my parents encouraged me to have an equal say. I guess that was partly because I grew up around adults, so I acted more like them than your average grade-school kid.

Dad and Mom agreed with me, but Doc seemed not to know what to do. I guess no matter how many degrees you have, sometimes you still don't know what to do. In the end, it's better to rely on your gut, if you ask me.

Later that day, Doc Alex told Champ that Joe the bartender wanted to offer him a job where he could make more money than he was making with his allowance. He and Miss Thelma would reduce his allowance, but working at the restaurant would give him more spending money in the long run.

Champ told his parents he'd try the job but only if his parents wouldn't nag him if he quit. Before his first day, Doc said he complained non-stop about how cleaning the toilets might make him barf. Miss Laura coached Champ on how to get the pee off the men's bathroom floor. He held his nose when he mopped, and eventually he got good at getting all the stains out. Bussing tables was a snap, and he loved it when customers told him he looked like a movie star and should sign up with a casting agency.

The one job he couldn't stand was washing dishes, but when Mom wasn't looking and he heard his favorite numbers playing on the jukebox, he danced around the kitchen like Elvis the Pelvis, wiggling his hips. He was a few years older than me, but I was secretly in love with him. Who wouldn't be when they saw how cool he looked in his black trousers with a pink stripe running down the sides and his DA (duck ass) haircut? Of course, he saw me as a bratty baby sister, but I could dream, couldn't I?

One thing I learned from Doc was that if you give your kids too much stuff, they won't love or respect you anymore. It only makes things worse. I think it's important for kids to depend on themselves and for parents not to hand them everything they want. I also learned that if you eat too many baskets of French fries, you   might gain a ton of weight like Doc. But there are a lot of worse things you could do because Doc was an ace. He always did his best to help his patients, and he loved us like we were his own family.

Years later, Doc Alex died of natural causes, whatever that is. He didn't die of eating too many fries and goodies like we all thought he would. He could have eaten all the fries and other fattening stuff he wanted and enjoyed his life more instead of worrying. That made me think about how we think one thing is going to get us, and in the end, something entirely different does us in. I guess it's best to not worry about the things we do, after all, because they're not the things that cause us to die.

I asked Dad if he'd heard how Champ was doing. Dad said that the last time he saw him was at Doc's memorial service. Champ said that working at the Royal Gardens gave him the sense of self-discipline he needed to turn his life around. He told my parents that (Eliminate that he was scheduled to graduate from college soon as a business major. He would have made Doc proud, I thought. Miss Thelma would be there to see him graduate from Temple University, Dad's alma mater.

Mom said Miss Thelma was still bitching and complaining, even at Doc's funeral—this time about the reckless limo driver who chauffeured her around and the overcooked roast beef at the funeral luncheon. But I knew the real reason. She missed Doc and wondered how she'd be able to go on without him.

Chapter Five
Take it Back!

"Life is a big crap shoot. There's no rhyme or reason to it. It's all random."
—Mr. Andy Galecki

During the second half of first grade, I came down with one childhood illness after another: measles, mumps, chicken pox, and scarlet fever— you name it. Mom faced rough days and nights between cooking banquets for the Kiwanis and Lions club and making sure I didn't die from any of these diseases, but I learned I faced something far worse than death. Our doctor, a withered old poop in a tweed suit, prescribed enemas to bring down the fevers, and Mom wouldn't let me escape until she carried out his command.

One night she ran after me, caught me and turned me over her knee to administer the dreaded enema from a contraption that looked like a hot water bottle and was called an enema bag. "It's for your own good," Mom said. "You could die from a high fever, and this is the only way we have to bring it down."

It's the first time she showed a side I didn't know she had, a forceful side that showed up whenever I had a high fever. I ran a lot of high fevers when I was growing up, so I learned to run fast when Mom took the enema bag out of the linen closet. Once, when I was eleven, she broke down the door in our new suburban home to force an enema on me.

"We have no choice. The fever's not coming down fast enough," she said.

She grabbed me, turned me over her knee, and the water started rushing into my butt until I screamed and almost passed out. The sensation of that soapy water flooding out my insides horrified me. After it was over, she said, "All that commotion for nothing. No more fever now."

Getting those enemas left me with a fear of all things anal. Mom always said she had no choice, but I believed there had to be a better, kinder, gentler way to bring down a fever.

As usual, Dad let her handle everything related to my illnesses, so he wasn't much help. "Can't you give her a laxative or something to bring the fever down instead of making her scream her head off like a maniac?" he said once when he heard all the noise. "The customers are asking what's going on up there. I don't want them to call the cops on us." And that was the end of it as far as Dad was concerned.

I had to stay home from school until I completely recovered from my illnesses. Mom decided, along with Miss Clara, to homeschool me. When I recovered, the school tested me in each subject to determine if I'd be re-admitted when the doctor said I was well enough to return to school. I have to admit I was afraid of the nuns because they hit the boys with a yardstick. Even though the girls only got a small tap on the wrist with a ruler, got their hair pulled, and were called "bold, brazen articles," I was still afraid of them, right up until eighth grade, when we graduated.

Dad relapsed further into depression when he had to take on some of Mom's jobs because she had to oversee my health care during my illnesses. Mom couldn't go with him to his therapy sessions because she had to take care of me in addition to her duties as chief cook and waitress in the restaurant. Without Mom attending the sessions, the doctors took it upon themselves to blame Mom for Dad's problems, saying it was due to lack of sexual desire on her part. I overheard Mom and Dad shouting one night in their bedroom. "Do you honestly believe that sex is the reason for your depression?" Mom asked.

"How the hell should I know?" Dad said. "I know that it sure is lonely without it."

Afraid that Mom would slow down on her work schedule, and not wanting to annoy her, Dad avoided talking about sex with her and going into a rage, as he often did when they disagreed. But Dad couldn't let it go, frustrated lawyer that he never became. "Maybe the doctors have a point," he said, which set her off big time.

"Well, go and find yourself a girlfriend like you did before, and see where *that* lands you," Mom said, ending the argument. Dad could never make it in the business without Mom's help, so she had the final word.

In the end, Dad got the guts to tell the psychiatrist that Mom wasn't the reason for the depression. And please don't call it *my* depression, he'd tell them, as he had nothing to do with it. It came from his ancestors, those who came before him, with a little craziness thrown in by his dear living relatives who were his mentors and role models. Dad knew how to make a case for himself. Even the doctors didn't know how to respond.

I never heard Dad and Mom argue about lack of sex being the cause of his mental illness again, so for all I knew, they had started doing it again, if they'd ever stopped in the first place. That was the last I heard them talk about it, but I'm sure they did. I figured they still must have done it because when I was sixteen Mom got pregnant with my sister. That made me certain that something was going on, if only for that one time.

Around this time, Andy Galecki became a regular at the bar. He was an attendant at Byberry and was bent over and wore red and blue checkered shirts every day. He coughed so much that Dad said if he didn't get help for his hacking, he'd have to stay in his rented room near the hospital because he'd scare away the customers who thought they might catch it. Andy said the cough was from smoking from the time he was thirteen, and he couldn't do anything about it. Could he please keep coming to the bar as he had no other friends but the guys at work, and Dad treated him so well he'd hate to be banned from the bar. Dad backed down and told me to treat Andy extra nicely when he came in.

One day, I found Mr. Galecki sitting on the step outside the bar's back door. He held his head in his bony hands. "Can I get you anything, Mr. Galecki?" I said.

"I'd like some strawberry ice cream, little one," he said in a raspy voice.

I ran to the restaurant walk-in box where they kept the big vats of ice cream. Vanilla fudge, chocolate, and strawberry. I scooped out a big helping of ice cream and put globs of homemade whipped cream on top that Mom had made to top her famous cheesecake. Oh, and I grabbed a maraschino cherry from a jar and topped the ice cream with it. Everybody should have a cherry on their ice cream, especially Mr. Galecki, because he always looked sad. Mom would have been annoyed about raiding the ice cream freezer, but I figured Mr. Galecki needed it more than her customers.

"Here's your ice cream," I said, handing it to Mr. Galeki like it was the crown jewels.

"Beautiful," he said. "This is a work of art, little one." He dug into his dessert like he was a doomed man eating his last meal. Then he handed me the empty dish and blew me a kiss.

I wasn't prepared for what happened next. Before I could ask how he liked the ice cream, his face got all white and pasty, his head rolled back, and he stared up at me with his sunken gray eyes that made him look like a mummy. I could only see the white parts of his eyes. Somehow, he made the blue parts disappear.

"This is how I'll look when I'm dead, little one. I'm not long for this world."

I'd never seen a dead person, and if this was what one looked like, I never wanted to again. "Take it back," I shouted. "Take it back." Dad and a couple of his customers, and even Miss Laura, heard my screams. She pushed open the door.

"What the hell did you say to frighten her like that, Andy?" Dad asked.

"Just telling her the truth, Joe. She has to learn these things. One day I'm here, and the next I won't be. Don't do no good to shield kids from the truth, does it?"

Dad helped him up and the other two guys pulled him into the dining room, which was empty by now. "I'll get him some coffee and some pie," Dad said.

"And here's a cool rag to wipe your face." Miss Laura said, running in after she heard me scream.

Miss Laura met my eyes with hers and said in a low voice. "I can see why you were scared, Miss Catherine. He looks like he escaped from that graveyard across the street."

Dad shot her a look. "Let's not be too descriptive, Miss Laura. We'll frighten her more." Miss Laura went off muttering to herself about how dumb white people could be sometimes.

"Thanks for the offer but forget that pie, Joe. I already had ice cream,"

Mr. Galecki said. "Don't want to eat up all your profits. You guys did enough for me already."

He looked up at me and smiled. His eyes were back to normal, and I could see the blue in them, thank God. It seemed like Miss Laura's cool rag had brought him back to life.

"Thanks for that ice cream, little one. It made my day," he said. "Sorry if I ruined yours. Didn't mean nothing by it, but I had to tell somebody, and you were the only one there. Even though you're a little kid, I believe you understand."

"It's okay, Mr. Galecki. I was pretty scared when you made yourself look dead," I said. "I've never seen a dead person, and I never want to, but I think you did a pretty good imitation of one."

Dad brought me upstairs so I could listen to my shows on the radio with Mom. They were a lot less scary than Mr. Galecki. That night, Mom and I didn't study math or reading. We listened to our shows and snuggled together. Tomorrow would be my first day of school after three months staying home.

The principal, Mother Mary Edmund, would give me tests in all my subjects to see how well Mom and Miss Clara had home-schooled me when I was sick. If they did a good job and I passed all my tests, I wouldn't have to repeat first grade. I asked the spirits in the Roosevelt Cemetery to help me, and I also asked Mother Mary, Jesus' mom, to help in case the spirits were busy that day helping some other kids, who needed them more.

As it turns out, I passed everything and aced all my tests. I was officially a second grader and that fall met my new teacher, Sister Marie Gabriel, a young nun with fifty kids in her class. She never yelled like some of the other nuns and gave you free pretzel sticks when you made the honor roll. I always wondered why the priests got their own cook and housekeeper, and the nuns had to take turns cooking and do their own laundry. Maybe that's why they were so snippy and took it out on their students.

Many of our customers, psychiatrists, and attendants like Andy Galecki, worked at Byberry Hospital. I often heard them talking in low tones about the ugly stuff that went on there. They said they tried to call these abuses to the management's attention and got nowhere. According to Dad's customers who worked at the hospital, Byberry was a house of horrors. Mr.

Cuff, Mr. Galecki, and Doctor Alex told stories about how some staff members abused patients. They told Dad how some attendants tied the patients to big blocks of ice and made them sit there for hours shivering until they calmed down and did what the attendants told them.

I could never picture my friends at the bar doing these terrible things I saw in the newspapers about Byberry. They swore they always treated the patients with respect. I believed them and so did Dad. He would have thrown them out of the bar if he thought they did anything to hurt people. That was one thing about Dad. Making money always took second place to doing what was right. When things weren't going well in the restaurant business, he never raised the prices. Dad loved his customers and treated them fairly even when it meant making less money.

My family was concerned about the reports about Byberry, but we didn't think Dad's customers were involved. As an adult, I read about some of the atrocities in a 1946 article in *The Philadelphia Record*. The author talked about the infamous water cure at Byberry in which an attendant caused a patient to become unconscious using soaked towels wrapped around their necks until they passed out from lack of oxygen.

An article called "Inside Byberry Mental Hospital," says that some of the most horrible abuses at the mental hospital happened when patients were treated for dental and medical problems. For example, dental workers pulled teeth without giving Novocain and did other procedures on patients' teeth without painkillers.

Byberry finally closed its doors in 1991. Sometimes, at night, as the Royal Gardens Sign swung back and forth, I heard the people in the Roosevelt cemetery calling to me about the tortured souls at Byberry. "The souls are at peace now in the ever after, no need to worry. Don't be afraid. It's all good."

I couldn't help but wonder if those patients still roamed those haunted grounds at Byberry. One part of me believed that my friends, Dr. Alex, Mr. Cuff, and Galecki, may have known what was going on and didn't say anything to their bosses, but I couldn't bear to think about it.

I hoped Mr. Galecki wouldn't die but I knew he would, and not because he made a spooky face and told me he would. I was becoming more psychic each day. I knew he would die in a couple of months, and he did.

Mom and Dad thought it would be best if I went to Mr. Galecki's funeral, and Mom bought me a new pink dress and a sparkly headband with socks to match. Mr. Galecki looked just like he did when he sat outside and asked for strawberry ice cream and then pretended he was dead. The people at the funeral home wrapped rosary beads around his fingers. I knew he wouldn't want them to do that because he had his own way of thinking, and it didn't include religion. "Life is a big crap shoot," he'd always say. "No rhyme or reason to it. It's all random." I wish I'd spent more time talking to him and offering him different flavors of ice cream with gobs of whipped cream and a cherry on top.

After the funeral they didn't have a luncheon, so Dad took our family out to "Cliff's Home of the French-Fried Hot Dog," and we pigged out on hot dogs, fries, and strawberry ice cream, of course, to remember Mr. Galecki. Cliff sweated into the food as usual, but no one said anything because he was one of Dad's good friends and neighbors. I started thinking about why people go out to eat after a funeral. Probably to make themselves feel better and remember the dead person in a happy way. It somehow didn't seem right to be eating and whooping it up after a funeral, but I loved the hot dogs and the ice cream.

I'll never understand why people have to suffer and die if I live to be one hundred and ten. I tried to believe in the Baltimore Catechism and what Miss Clara taught me about the angels and saints and how they watched over us, but sometimes I wondered how much of it was true because it didn't seem that everything happened for a reason, like the nuns and priest said.

Why would a baby be born only to die from a serious illness before they've had a chance to live? Why are so many people killed in earthquakes or tsunamis when they never did anything to meet such a horrible end? I'll never figure it out, at least, not in this life. Maybe someday we'll all find out. For now, I try not to think about it and hope somebody's watching over us and cares about what happens to us. Do you wonder about these things too?

There are also so many things I don't understand that people do. When Mom gave me enemas to bring my fevers down, I didn't understand how she could have changed from the best mother in the world I listened to our radio shows with and how we cried at night together when Dad came in from bar-hopping at 2:00 AM. Mom became a different person when she screamed at me and forced that soapy stuff into my butt, but I guess she was desperate for me to get better. I eventually did, even though it left its scars. I forgive her for that; she probably doesn't remember doing it, especially in heaven where she lives now. Everything is supposed to be perfect there, and people do their best to make things right in the ever after.

When I took my tests to enter second grade, I was happy I passed all of them; I did best in English and religion. Miss Clara, the waitress, knew enough about the Catholic catechism to become a certified Catholic, but I could tell she didn't like any church because she left the non-denominal one she belonged to when they started begging for more money.

I heard her talking to Mom once about how she could never become a Catholic because she didn't like their strict rules about birth control and how you had to wait until it was safe, according to some dumb calendar to have sex, or you might have a baby. She called it "the rhythm method." They both laughed about it and Mom said it was "Vatican Roulette," whatever the heck that meant.

I didn't understand what that conversation was about being a kid and all, but I wondered why the church would stick their nose in places it didn't belong. I still don't know, except maybe to sign up new members from all the new babies being born because "rhythm" didn't always work. Sounded dumb to me then and now. Nobody should be able to tell people what to do in their personal lives, not even the Church.

I liked the rest of the things Miss Clara taught me about angels and saints and how they look out for us when we're going through rough times. Mother Mary, Christ's mom, always said we could come to her if we had a problem, and she always seemed to answer me when I prayed to her. I also liked the idea of the Ten Commandments because they made it easy to see what kinds of things pissed God off and threw us out of His good graces.

One thing I didn't like was picturing God as a grumpy old man with white whiskers who made people die for no reason whenever he felt like it. I'll never understand that. I wondered then as I do now what his purpose was in creating the earth and all those beautiful people if they were going to suffer and die. I imagine our brains are not big enough to understand why so many sad things happen to the people He created. I try not to think it about it too much or I'll go crazy. I swear I will.

Chapter Six
The Pixilated Sisters left off.

"I want a brassiere and a girdle..."
—me to Mom after I coveted her undies

My father's two unmarried sisters, Aunt Minnie and Aunt Mary, lived at my grandparents' farmhouse, which we got to by running across the tomato patch in back of the bar. I also had an Uncle Louie (Dad's brother), but didn't have much contact with him growing up. He lived with his wife and two daughters, worked as a law clerk, and wore tailor-made suits, while his wife wore pretty, but plain, department store dresses. From what I've seen, he and Dad treated their wives the same. They expected them to give everything they had to the relationship and to get little in return.

I enjoyed seeing Uncle Louie and his family at Nan Nan's Sunday dinners. He was funny and kind to all of us and. taught me the joys of eating a meatball sandwich with lettuce drenched in Italian dressing on a big chunk of crispy Italian bread from Lanza's bakery. He, like my dad, majored in law and worked in the field all his life.

As kids, my brother Joe and I spent hours at the farmhouse with my grandparents, Uncle Tony, and my two single aunts. Mom called the ladies "The Pixilated Sisters." She christened her eccentric sisters-in-law with *pixilated,* the name of the wifty sisters who originally acted in a vaudeville show Mom had heard about that became a great success. The two actresses got together again in 1938 in a hit movie called "Mr. Deeds Goes to Town," and they made the pixilated sisters famous. That's how Mom pictured my two aunts. To her, they acted like the silly sisters in that movie.

Mom called my aunts the name behind their backs because she'd never tell them to their faces that she thought they were somewhat odd. She felt it fit them perfectly. Most of the time, they seemed clueless, but they held regular jobs. Mom didn't tell my father what she'd named them because he'd jump to their defense. He thought all his relatives were perfect, even when they did stuff like shoot a rifle in the air with a little kid nearby when they were drunk, which is exactly what Pop Pop did once.

After a few years, Aunt Minnie and Aunt Mary moved to a rowhouse in Northeast Philly, along with Uncle Tony. Aunt Minnie, whose real name was Philomena, worked as a keypunch operator at Frank and Seder department store in the center of the city, and Mary, her older sister, commuted to Temple University from the farmhouse to earn her degree in secondary education. After graduation, Aunt Mary worked as an English, French, and Spanish teacher. My grandparents loved both sisters but treated Mary like her royal highness (Minnie called her the "royal hiney.") Minnie, who scrubbed the floors on her hands and knees, was treated like Cinderella by my grandparents.

Because Mary had earned a college degree and had a professional job, her parents felt she shouldn't do any dirty work around the house, like mopping the floor or cleaning toilets. Being a college graduate was important to my grandparents who emigrated from Italy and wanted all their kids to have their degree so they could go out and make their mark on the world.

Aunt Minnie was the sweet sister, while Aunt Mary was the strict, mean one. One fall day, when red, yellow, and orange leaves carpeted the farm, Aunt Minnie raced across the field with me riding piggyback. When I was about six, I started screaming like a banshee in the middle of Happy Hour at the bar: "I want a brassiere and a girdle, big ones, just like Mom." I'd seen Mom ironing her intimates (in those days you ironed everything). I wanted a pair of my own underwear, and nothing was going to stop me, even though I was little and had nothing to fill the bra like Mom did with her Playtex 38 D.

Mom hurriedly dug up my red two-piece bathing suit and told Aunt Minnie to tell me it was a real bra and girdle like Mom's and to get me the heck out of the bar pronto. Aunt Minnie helped me change into the bra and girdle in her fancy bedroom at the farmhouse, but she carried me back to the bar screaming, "I want a brassiere and a girdle." She couldn't fool me. I could tell it wasn't the real thing. For one thing, I had no boobs (*bosoms* according to Mom) and no big hips for the girdle to hold in.

The customers at the bar got a good laugh out of my dramatic performance. Mom always compared me to Sarah Bernhardt and said I could easily have a career as an actress. As punishment for throwing that scene at the bar, I had to sit in the corner of the dining room for fifteen minutes with a dunce cap on my curly brown hair. Instead of dunce, it said *Sarah Bernhardt*. I'd rather be a great actress than a dunce, any day. Nobody thought the punishment fit the crime, least of all Miss Clara and Miss Laura. They both said they would have given me a good walloping, but that would have gotten me more sympathy from the patrons, who loved my antics so much they ordered another round of beers and pigs in blankets, which they only usually got during the World Series because Mom said they were a pain to make.

Another time Aunt Minnie carried me piggyback (to the bar this time) was when Pop Pop worked himself into a rage. That usually happened after he'd had more than a few beers. "Pop Pop's mad," my aunt would say in a shaky voice. "Pop Pop's mad." That was the signal for me to stand on a kitchen chair and hop on her back for the ride back to the bar.

One spring day, Pop Pop was in rare form. I was standing out on the porch with him admiring the tomato plants, and a man started shooting at him with a rifle from across the field shouting, "Dago, go home. We don't want you here, you dirty wop." Pop shouted back at him in Italian and fired his hunting rifle into the air, even though I was standing next to him. Aunt Minnie stormed out the front door and shouted at Pop Pop to put down the damn gun and took his beer can and emptied it on the ground.

Once again, she carried me back to the bar on her bony hunched back. "Why is Pop Pop so mad? What's a dago and a wop?" I asked.

"They're nasty names for Italians. When people hate each other, they'll find any excuse to call each other bad names," Aunt Minnie answered. The man who called Pop Pop names came from another country too, but he got here before Pop Pop,, so I guess he thought that made it ok to call him awful names.

"I'm glad I heard that ruckus or you could have gotten hurt, Cathedral." Aunt Minnie loved to make up weird names for me like *Cathedral*. I liked Uncle Tony's name, *Catty School,* better because I knew I'd be a teacher one day plus it didn't sound ridiculous like *Cathedral*.

From then on, Mom rarely let me go to the farmhouse without her. When Pop Pop started drinking, there was no telling what could happen.

Aunt Minnie was known for doing Pixilated things, like the times she scrubbed the basement and kitchen floors until they got holes in them. If Uncle Tony dropped Fig Newton crumbs near his cubby, she'd rush to sweep them up, fearing a mouse might find them before she did.

"Mini-ooch," Tony would say, with the accent on the last syllable, calling her his favorite name for her, "Stop working so hard or you're going to get sick, and I'll get stuck taking care of you."

"Oh, stuff it up your fat ass, Tony," she'd shoot back. She was sweet to all of us, but she could also cuss crazier than the guys at the bar, especially when Tony got on her nerves, which was most of the time.

One day a neighbor, Mrs. Dill, who was about 90, brought over a beautiful vanilla cake with milk chocolate icing. Aunt Minnie gushed over it and said she couldn't wait to taste it. The minute Mrs. Dill left, my aunt opened up the garbage can with her toes, and plop, in went the cake. It made a loud thud.

"Why did you do that? I wanted that cake so badly," I said, tears forming in my eyes.

Aunt Minnie scrunched up her nose like she did whenever she talked about germs. "I never eat anything from someone else's kitchen We have no way of knowing how clean it is. Maybe they have cockroaches crawling around or mouse droppings," she said, wrinkling her nose in disgust.

"Well, I want some of that cake," I said in a snotty voice, but Aunt Minnie ignored me like she always did when I wasn't my usual sweet self. When Aunt Minnie wasn't looking, I fished a huge chunk of the cake out of the garbage. There weren't any worms or slimy stuff in there, so I figured it was ok. The cake tasted sweet and moist, and the icing was rich and buttery, better than I thought it would be, better than bakery cake, which I loved.

The next time I saw Mrs. Dill, I asked her for the recipe so Mom could make it for us. But I didn't tell her that Aunt Minnie threw her cake in the garbage. She would never have spoken to my aunt again. Mom made that cake for us many times, and Aunt Minnie never guessed it was the same one Mrs. Dill made that she threw in the garbage.

Despite her eccentricities, Aunt Minnie presented herself as a sweet lady in a flowered house dress and wildly permed salt-and-pepper hair with bright red lipstick that bled beyond her natural lip line. She always stashed away candy and cookies for when Joe and I came to visit. Once Aunt Mary caught her giving my brother candy and she flipped out. "He'll get fat if you feed him that. He's chubby enough." Then she pushed a peeled overripe banana in his face. "Eat this, you'll love it," Aunt Mary said.

Joe gagged the mushy banana down because Aunt Mary called the shots, and Aunt Minnie never had the last word when it came to us kids. Unlike Mom and Aunt Minnie, Aunt Mary graduated from Temple University, which wasn't as good as Penn in Dad's eyes, but it qualified her to proclaim the truth on everything from politics (Republicans were always better than Democrats until JFK came along) to raising kids.

After Aunt Mary landed a job at Seaview High School near Atlantic City, New Jersey, she moved to a rooming house near the seashore. Mom said she styled her hair like George Washington and didn't wash it after she had it washed and set at Edna's beauty shop until it was time for the next visit six weeks later. Aunt Mary said she wouldn't know how to style it right, so she'd rather leave it that way until she met up with Edna, her stylist, again. Her hair was a real grease pit, and her students razzed her about it.

Chapter Seven
Emergency, Emergency!

Mary: "Stop feeding the kids sweets, Minnie. You don't use your brain. It will stunt their growth."
Minnie: "Shut the hell up, Mary. Just because you went to college doesn't mean you know anything about kids."
—Aunt Minnie and Aunt Mary going at it

Toward the end of her 25-year career at Seaview, Aunt Mary started losing control of her class. Maybe she got burned out, the kids were harder to handle, or she got tired of teaching kids who found French, Spanish, and English completely irrelevant to their lives. Before things fell apart, she'd been a highly regarded faculty member that younger teachers looked up to as their mentor.

In the final months of her career, her students used to say that Aunt Mary was a *trip*. They never knew what to expect or how she'd react to their pranks. One day a couple of her wild students proclaimed that Mary had purple hair. (Of course they were lying. She had greasy black hair.) Mary immediately got on the PA system and shouted for help from anyone who would listen. "Emergency, emergency, emergency! Principal to room 204."

As Aunt Mary told it, the kids banged on their desks and howled, and teachers peeked out of nearby classrooms to see what Mary's latest emergency was as she made a habit of shouting into the public address system when she couldn't control her class.

The principal and vice principal, who were aware of Mary's dramatic pleas for help in a school overrun with kids who loved to get over on their teachers, came running to Room 204. They found the students dancing on the desktops and singing, "Miss Mary has purple hair."

Aunt Mary told me how proud she was that she greeted the administrators in her harshest tone. "What the hell took you so long? I thought you'd take forever to get here. These kids are out of control. I demand suspension for all of them."

Principal Biggins clapped her hands twice and then three more times to get the kids' attention. "Listen up. I need you to get back to your seats. Show your teacher some respect. This isn't how we behave at Seaview High." Surprisingly, and because the principal was over six feet tall, weighed a couple hundred pounds, and had a deep voice like a fog horn, they listened– but only until next time when the kids let a burlap sack of mice loose in my aunt's classroom, and all hell broke loose. Mary was more terrified of the critters than her kids, and she ended up running out the door and leaving the kids to fend for themselves.

After the mouse episode, the principal called the school police to restore order. Principal Biggins told Aunt Mary that maybe a suburban school would suit her personality better. Although she was forced to resign, she found a job almost immediately, thanks to her academic credentials (she could teach three languages), and the fact that Mom and Dad knew the superintendent and his wife who used to come to the restaurant. They were happy to put in a good word for her with the principal of the local high school.

Principal Biggins didn't tell the school about Mary's discipline problems because she wanted her to leave her school as soon as possible; she also knew my aunt wouldn't get a job if she told the district about her issues with the students. Aunt Mary and the whole family were thrilled that she got a job in the Pennsylvania school district where I later attended high school, about twenty miles from Philly.

The principal at Seaview must have felt sorry for her, so she gave her a pretty good recommendation despite her problems. She called her a genius and a scholar but didn't mention her lousy classroom management skills. Aunt Mary found out early on that the kids in her new school acted out even worse than her Seaville students did. They made fun of her clothes and talked and laughed non-stop in her classroom, despite her pleas to give her a chance and show her some common courtesy. It didn't help that the students loved the popular teacher she took over for when she was forced to retire due to illness.

The kids at Aunt Mary's new school loved to gossip about how she switched off between two skirts and two blouses every other day and wore the same shoes every day. "Miss S., why don't you splurge on some new outfits?" they'd taunt her. "You look like an old lady wearing those ugly skirts down to your ankles, and don't even talk to me about those penny loafers. They make you look like a patient in a nursing home."

Aunt Mary was shocked and dismayed by the students' reactions and didn't know what to do. She knew she couldn't continue teaching because it had become unbearable. She wondered if it was totally her fault or if there was a new breed of student who simply couldn't respond to her reasonable requests to listen up and pay attention. Who knew?

Mary tried everything to restore order in her new classroom, including writing reams of pink slips, threatening kids with detention, calling homes, and flicking the lights off and on. Alas, nothing worked, and she went home in tears every night. She was an expert in her subjects, but she couldn't control her classes.

A concerned assistant principal sat in her classes and offered suggestions, like singling out the most uncontrollable kid in the class or offering rewards for good behavior, but nothing worked, and he told her that maybe she was burned out or not cut out for teaching. Finally, she quit but had earned enough money from her previous job to support herself with a small pension and the fact that she hoarded all her money. She said it was too late to start over in a new career.

Aunt Mary was glad to move back to the shore because her fiancé Joshua Portman lived there, and carrying on a long-distance romance was hard. Before she met Josh when she was eating in a local restaurant, she had one other serious boyfriend when she was in her twenties, named Carter, who was a Temple medical student. They were engaged, deeply in love, and had planned to marry soon.

One day, when Carter was crossing the hazardous Roosevelt Boulevard, a car ran over him. He was killed instantly. Aunt Mary vowed she'd never get involved romantically after she lost Carter, but about thirty years later, she met Josh and fell in love again.

Josh worked as Postmaster in a small seashore town and made a good salary. He spent most of his money courting Mary at their favorite restaurant,

Mac's, in Ocean City and taking her to other fine restaurants in the area, like Chi Chi's and The Knife and Fork Inn in Atlantic City.

Mom called their love affair a storybook romance. They both lived in different rooming houses at the shore, and both took cabs to Mac's because they didn't drive. They showed up at the restaurant every Friday around the same time. One night they looked at each other "across a crowded room" just like in the song "Some Enchanted Evening" sung by Frank Sinatra and Ezio Pinza. The rest is history.

Aunt Mary was blown away with Josh's adoration of her and the fact that he wrote her romantic sonnets that would rival Shakespeare's; he loved her lively personality and exotic good looks. They got engaged after a brief courtship, and after they married, she moved into a Cape Cod house with Josh, became a housewife and volunteered at Corpus Christi Church in nearby Linwood. She finally found her niche and never set foot in a classroom again.

Mary and Josh married in a Catholic Mass with Aunt Minnie and me in attendance as maid-of-honor and bridesmaid respectively. Mary wore a white silk gown trimmed with Alencon lace. A rhinestone tiara topped her George Washington long-layered bob, which Edna, her stylist, had finally washed and set for the big day.

Aunt Minnie and I wore blue velvet floor length dresses and tiny blue hats that sat atop our heads like little pies to match our dresses. We carried dyed blue carnations, and Mary carried white ones, a flower whose smell I've always hated. Mary said the carnations wouldn't die before the ceremony was over, like roses would, so they were good enough for her.

Her nerves veered out-of-control before her wedding, and she spent a couple of hours that should have been happy ones berating Angelina, an elderly cousin, who had graciously offered
her help with her gown and veil as she dressed for the ceremony. Aunt Mary picked away at her mercilessly until Angelina left in tears. "You didn't fix my train right and I hate how you messed up my hairstyle that Edna worked on for so long to make me look beautiful."

I had to smile at the irony at seeing Aunt Mary on the happiest day of her life dressed like an angel acting like the bride from hell, screaming at her poor cousin like she was her maid servant. It reminded me of how Aunt Mary sometimes treated Aunt Minnie. I wondered if Aunt Mary suffered from the same mood swings that plagued my father. Maybe that's why, as she got older, she faced so many problems in her teaching job.

Aunt Mary was a strict Catholic, who once remarked to Mom that the young wives who went up to the altar to receive Communion were probably practicing birth control. She considered that a mortal sin that would damn you to hell forever. Of course, Mary was past fifty when she married, so she never had to worry about the fate of a sperm meeting up with an egg, thank God, the angels and saints, and all the Popes who ever lived.

Mary always idolized my father, who went to an Ivy League college. Uncle Tony took trips to the store to buy groceries for her and Minnie after Mary moved back home for a short time because of her new job. He kept a watchful eye on the cabins and the farmhouse when no one was home. Tony was famous for "watching the house." Mary couldn't stand some of his strange habits like doing Relsteen rituals, never seeing a doctor when he got sick, and not letting anyone who had a dog enter the house. He was her big brother, and she did her best to get along with him even though she thought he was batshit crazy.

During Tony's last illness, he wouldn't let the nurses touch him for fear he'd catch germs, even though they wore gloves and masks. Mary got up in the nurse's face and said, "He's a simpleton and doesn't understand how to act, so please humor him. Talk to him like he's a little kid and he'll respond better."

Once, Tony refused to buy a bunch of bananas from a guy in the Italian market because they touched his stomach that stuck out under his wife beater. Who knows what germs you could catch from that big hairy stomach, especially when the guy had disgusting BO, which bothered Tony who put deodorant on three times a day, just in case.

Sometimes Uncle Tony knew more than Aunt Mary did, like after the Doc said Minnie had dementia, and Tony took care of her by buying her food, giving her meds, and sweeping up the little turds that leaked out of her panties onto the floor of the basement where my aunt and uncle spent all their time after Minnie retired from Frank and Seder. The company gave her a party and a shiny new Timex watch. It was the happiest day of her life, and she raved about it for years.

You could always find Nan Nan and Pop Pop on the couch in the basement of their northeast Philly rowhouse. The only time they went upstairs was when they went to bed. You could always count on seeing Uncle Tony in his cubby surrounded by Fig Newtons with all his test papers spread out, ready for me to mark, and my grandparents sitting on either end of the couch until the day they died.

The rest of the three-story house looked like one of those mausoleums at the Roosevelt Cemetery. It was spotless with all the scrubbing Minnie did and the fact that my relatives went up the steep steps to the second floor only to cook, and to the third floor only to sleep.

No one ever set foot in the living room or dining room, and if company came, they sat in the basement with my grandparents and aunts eating macaroni, dipping their Italian bread in the tomato gravy, and reminiscing about times gone by. Before Minnie got sick, she and my grandparents listened to the Italian hour on the radio, drank coffee and ate Biscotti.

When Mary moved back to the farm for her new job, she spent her time reading, marking papers, which the kids threw in the trash as soon as they got them, or gabbing with Josh non-stop on the phone. It was long distance, so Pop Pop blew up when he saw the bill and made her pay it.

It was a good thing she married Josh and moved back to the shore, or Aunt Minnie might have had to carry me as teenager piggy-back to the bar and scream, "Pop Pop's mad." That would have killed her back, which was, by now, already totally bent over like The Hunchback of Notre Dame.

I learned many lessons from my aunts. From Aunt Minnie I learned that our life's worth should be measured by how kind we act toward people and not how many degrees we have or where we went to college. Aunt Minnie had a knack for making me and my brother feel comfortable asking her questions about anything, and she always had candy bars (Hershey's with almonds) in her pocket and gave them to us when Aunt Mary wasn't around for fear of getting into a shouting match like this one.

Mary: "Stop feeding the kids sweets, Minnie. You don't use your brain. It will stunt their growth."

Minnie: "Shut the hell up, Mary. Just because you went to college doesn't mean you know anything about kids."

Mary: "That's why they always come to see you and ignore me. You're a big pushover and they know it, Minnie."

Minnie (grinning): "But who do they like better?"

Mary: "When they get older, they'll see you for who you are, a foolish old woman in a housedress and false teeth who worked as a keypunch operator and scrubbed the floors until they got holes in them."

Damn, Mary always got the last word, but Minnie didn't care, and neither did I. That's not to say that I didn't learn anything from Aunt Mary. She taught me to go after what I wanted and to study subjects that held my interest, like English and Spanish. And that's exactly what I did, graduating from Temple, her alma mater, and becoming a teacher as she did. I'm sorry she was beaten down by the kids and the system.

Maybe she was out of touch with a changing society and couldn't tolerate the kids any longer. Maybe she was burned out but didn't have anywhere to turn when she started having discipline problems. Possibly, if she'd taught in a college, where she'd face fewer classroom management issues, she would have found more satisfaction in her career as she grew older.

I also learned from Aunt Mary how important it is to find the love of your life as she did with Josh. She loved him more as they grew older together and always complimented him on the beautiful poems he wrote for her. She cherished her twenty years with him living at the Jersey shore in their little bungalow. He bought her carnations (her favorite) every week and pampered her with pretty dresses, but most of all, he loved discussing world affairs with her (he was a diehard Democrat, but it didn't bother her even though Richard Nixon was her hero).

After Josh died, Aunt Mary lived well into her nineties and was able to care for herself with a little help from Our Mother of Sorrows Catholic church's youth organization, whose teenaged volunteers brought her hot dogs with sauerkraut, soda, and homemade cupcakes regularly. She still took the cab to Mac's restaurant on the weekends, where the staff knew and loved her and reminisced with her about bygone days when she and Josh had their date nights, where they ate, danced, hugged, and kissed, in public, God forbid. Josh was always her one true love, the one that every person on this earth should meet before they die and remain faithful to forever after.

Aunt Minnie never had that experience, although one day she posed for a picture in a lacy wedding gown and elegant veil on the lawn of the Roosevelt Cemetery. I still have that picture. One night I dreamed (or was it real?) that the souls of the dead said how beautiful Minnie looked as a bride and that maybe she'd meet someone someday in the spirit world who would love her forever. If anyone deserved it, Aunt Minnie did.

Chapter Eight
A Dog, a Cat, and a Tree for Me

"Don't threaten my dad. You need to do what he says."
—me to an unruly customer

When I was a child living at the bar, you never knew how my dad was going to react because of his bipolar illness. One minute he'd be up, joking and telling stories with his cronies at the bar. Other times, he'd be down, bitching and complaining to Mom about how she came on to the ugly guys at the bar (she never did!).

When he got into his moods, Dad would berate me about how I always got in the way when he and his friends discussed private stuff that little girls shouldn't ask about, like how hot some ladies were who came into the bar or dumb stuff like sports scores they liked to bet on. He couldn't help it. He was never satisfied with how Mom and I acted, but I believe it was his illness kicking in and smacking us in the butt non-stop.

He rarely acted that way with his friends. They usually only saw his happy face, always ready to help with any problem or obstacle they faced. With Mom and me it was different. I guess he felt if he acted that way with his friends, they wouldn't stand by him like we did. Sometimes he could be warm and loving with me and Mom as he was when he told the guys at the bar to keep their voices down: Howdy Doody was coming on TV and my little girl loves that show, or when he showered Mom with pretty negligees from the lingerie store for no reason at all. You never knew how he'd react, and that was hard to take.

One of the things that got me through the rough times growing up were the two stray pets that came into my life through the kitchen entrance of the Royal Gardens. We called our first pet Suzie Gray or Eddie because we never knew whether the gray tabby mongrel was male or female. Suzy Gray, aka Eddie, came around early in the morning, loved to play catch with me after school, and lived on scraps from Mom's culinary creations. For the first few months, I switched between calling the cat Suzy Gray and Eddie. I'd call her and she'd answer to both names. "Here, Suzie, Suzie, Suzie. Here, Eddie, Eddie, Eddie." and she'd come running and latch on to my leg. After a while, Mom and Dad established that she was Suzie, although you couldn't quite tell from her private parts, Doc Alex verified it and said there was no mistaking she was female, and from then on, she was Suzie.

Suzie must have been conflicted about her sexual identity, but it didn't stop her from getting what she wanted. She especially loved Mom's tender roast beef dripping with gravy with chopped up roasted potatoes on the side. Tuna fish from a can made her purr like a motor and salivate. If you scratched behind her ears, she'd jump up on your lap, curl into a ball, and stay there for the night.

She arched her back and swiped at me when she didn't get what she wanted, mainly, my scruffy stuffed elephant, but mostly, she smiled, purred, and cuddled in my lap, which sent me to heaven. Mom explained how we had to have Suzy spayed and said how she might not be herself for a while. I bundled her up in a blanket to visit the vet who assured us she'd be fine.

Shortly after we got home from the vet's, she puked all over my bed. I stayed up with her and sang Elvis Presley's "Love Me Tender" to her until I thought she felt better. By the next morning, she was purring, kneading the rug, and looking for her roast beef dinner and cat treats for dessert. The only thing she didn't like was Italian food. It may have been the garlic. Dad started calling her Merigan" and said we'd better not tell Pop Pop about her food foibles, or he might shoot his rifle on the porch to scare her. Pop Pop didn't like anybody, even cats, ragging on Italians, and he let them know it pronto.

Suzy would take off down the highway for days for no reason at all other than to chase mice or get a change of scene, but then when she'd had enough time on the road, she'd show up at the pavement outside the restaurant and pace back and forth until we saw her and dished out chopped up chicken livers with gravy, her third favorite meal.

When Miss Clara taught me Catechism, Suzie Gray would hop up on my lap and meow like crazy. She especially like the stories about Jesus healing all the sick people and tried to eat a page of my Children's Bible. Although Dad wasn't a cat person, he tolerated her because he knew how much I loved her.

One day Dad sat me down and said that it was important not to get too attached to pets because they didn't live as long as people. Also, we lived on the Superhighway, where cars whizzed by and didn't stop for people or animals. I told dad that I'd always take care of Suzy and do my best not to let her out of my sight, which was no easy task. I always knew when she had the urge to roam because she got this crazy look in her eye and started ignoring me a few days before it happened. I think she felt guilty.

For once I had to admit that Dad was right. After we had Suzy for about two years, she didn't return to our kitchen door. Mom sent Dad out in his shiny blue Chrysler to comb the neighborhood. Mom and I even walked around all the graves and mausoleums in the Roosevelt Cemetery, calling out, "Suzy Gray," but we didn't find her there or at any other of her favorite places like Cliff's, Home of the French-Fried Hot Dog. She liked hanging out there because Cliff indulged her passion for hot dogs and fries. He even found a couple of mice for her out by the garbage cans. She jumped on them, tried to make their ends quick and painless, and gulped them down in a flash, leaving no earthly remains. It made me feel like barfing, if you want to know the truth.

When we didn't find Suzy, it ripped me apart. Even cuddling my stuffed elephant didn't console me. I regret not letting Suzy play with her often, but Mom told me I couldn't mope around over Suzy forever. It wouldn't bring her back. Mom and I made a collage of pictures of me with Suzy and talked about all the funny things she did and how she used to growl and swat us when we got on her nerves.

We had a ceremony for her even though we weren't sure if she was lost or dead. Miss Clara and I said a couple of Catholic prayers like "May the perpetual light shine upon you," at a little shrine I made with daisies and violets and pretty stones I found on the pavement outside the Royal Gardens. We also said a couple of Jewish prayers for good measure like, "May her memory be a blessing." I hoped the souls in the Roosevelt Jewish Cemetery would help watch over her because they visited me on a regular basis.

We also said "Angel of God, my guardian dear," and prayed the angels would take Suzie to heaven and the "Our Father," knowing it was Jesus' favorite prayer to his father. If that didn't take her straight to heaven, nothing would. I personally believe that pets belong in heaven, probably more than people do. They're never mean on purpose even though they hiss, growl and swat your hand when they get annoyed. Most times, they always know when you're feeling crappy and try their best to comfort you. That's why everybody should have a pet.

After Suzie disappeared, I swore I never wanted another pet. I felt so sad and lonely that even when Mom made me Campbell's vegetable soup, which I loved better than her homemade vegetable soup, I refused to eat it. Even vanilla fudge ice cream with salty pretzel sticks to dip in didn't make me feel better. I cried so much Mom made me talk to Father Houlihan, one of the priests from Our Lady of Grace church, who came in once in a while at lunchtime to escape the terrible cook at the rectory, for a beer and a meatball sandwich with melted mozzarella cheese.

Father told me there are many changes that happen in life and that we have to adjust to them and accept them or we'll live a miserable life. He reminded me St. Francis himself said to accept the things we cannot change. Easy for him to say—Francis was a saint, for God's sake. Father also told me that nothing lasted forever and that we have to learn not to get too attached to the things of the world. *Poop* is what I say to that. I even said it out loud, which really pissed him off.

After I listened to him blather on, I told him I didn't like what he said one bit, and if that's what a Catholic believed I might just turn into a heathen. That's what they called people who didn't believe in the church's teachings, so I guess I was a heathen, or maybe even an atheist. Father Houlihan couldn't believe what he was hearing, especially the poop part, and he gave me a good talking to.

He said that if I were his child, he'd turn me over his knee and spank me. After he finished, Mom lectured me about how I should never talk back to a priest because he represented Christ on earth. I said *poop* again, and Mom told me to go upstairs to my room. Father Houlihan still stopped by the bar occasionally for his usual beer and meatball sandwich with mozzarella cheese but did his best to avoid me. I guess he couldn't stay away from Mom's cooking and a nice, cold Bud. He told Mom she needed to teach me to have respect for my elders. Mom listened to him but admitted she'd made a mistake having him talk to me. He didn't have any kids, so it was hard for him to understand them. Priests weren't allowed to get married or have kids. What a dumb rule.

A few months after Suzy Gray, my cat, took off, another pet appeared at the kitchen door, this time a mixed-breed dog, mainly white with floppy black ears. He limped, so we called him Skipper. One happy spring day, he stood outside the kitchen door, begging to come in and eat whatever we had to offer. Mom was making Salisbury steaks and scalloped potatoes for a ladies' luncheon. When she saw I'd let the dog in, she mixed the meat and potatoes together and offered them to him.

Wow! Skipper lapped her food up like he'd never tasted anything so delicious. He ate at a fast and furious rate, more than I'd seen Doc gobble up Mom's fries. From that day on, Skipper never left our house. We bought him a collar with his name and took him to the vet, who proclaimed him fit and healthy. Skipper Spinelli became an official family member on that day and never left our side for the three years we had him.

Skipper was a great asset to the Royal Gardens. He was an amazing watchdog who barked at night if someone came within a quarter mile of our house. Dad ushered him into the bar if any of the guys (and sometimes ladies) got rowdy and started looking for a fight. Skipper stood by and bared his crooked teeth, growling his scary growl at whoever was threatening to beat up a love rival and refuse to leave the bar if the customers were drinking too much or giving Dad a hard time.

One time this man, Jimmy Porter, came into the bar threatening to beat up my dad. Dad told him to leave because he had too many drinks at some other bar before he came to The Royal Gardens. His breath reeked of booze, and he slurred his words. I hopped up on a bar stool and got right in Jimmy's face and said in my meanest voice, "Don't threaten my dad, Mister. You need to do what he says."

Dad moved me out of the way and later told me never to talk to those guys when they were drunk (I could tell right away if they were drunk by smelling the booze on their breath, plus they sounded weird when they talked. You didn't have to be psychic to know that, even if you were a kid).

I thought Skipper was going to tear the guy to bits the way he went after him, pulling on his pant leg, ripping it with his teeth, and barking up a storm. Dad and I let him rage on for a while to scare Jimmy until he begged us to call that damn dog off him. He got the message. We never saw Jimmy again after I told him off, and Skipper showed him he could take him down with no trouble.

When the attendants at Byberry had a rough day, Skipper jumped up on a stool to lick their faces or make funny noises to console them. To Dad, our dog was better than any psychiatrist, jumping up on all fours to greet him when he woke up, and cocking his head and making sad sounds when he sensed Dad wasn't at his best.

After Skipper became sure of himself, he started going for long walks, and we couldn't keep him away from the Superhighway, the most dangerous road in Bucks County. He knew his way home and always returned by dinnertime. One day he didn't come home on time, so Dad and I linked arms and crossed the highway with cars roaring by and barely missing us. I thought for sure we'd get killed and end up living with the spirits in the Roosevelt Cemetery. I was honestly shaking. Mom never found out or she would have had a conniption.

I told Dad to check the cemetery first because if I were a dog I'd want to explore a quiet, peaceful place where no one would call you out for being on their property. And that's exactly where we found him. He was having a grand old time sniffing around the gravestones and the flowers and growling at the dead guys in the cemetery. He didn't seem to notice us as we crept up on him and acted all nonchalant, like he didn't care if he went home with us. Dad and I put on his leash and dragged him home grumbling and growling. I guess he was having loads of fun roaming around with the spirits. Darned if I could figure it out.

All I know is he ate two platters of chopped up hamburger and mashed potatoes with onion gravy. He ate so fast he gagged and wretched and threw up all over the back porch. He could really make a pig of himself sometimes. Of course, I had to clean it up. Mom said that having a pet comes with responsibilities, and they always seemed to fall on me. That night he slept in my bed and listened to the Royal Gardens sign outside my window going *Whee Woo, Whee Woo.* I wonder if the spirits from the cemetery said anything to him about not going far from home because he never visited them again, at least not that I know of.

I thought Skipper had learned his lesson after getting lost in the cemetery, but after a couple months, he decided to go off on his own again. We drove up and down the Superhighway in either direction calling out to him from our car. People driving by must have thought we'd lost it. We stopped every so often and shouted his name, "Skipper, Skipper," but he wasn't around. A young police officer patrolling the area offered to help find him, but he had to leave quickly to go out on a call about a stolen car.

We travelled all the way to the Langhorne Speedway, where people drove for miles to watch car races, and when we didn't find him, we headed out to northeast Philly where Nan Nan and Pop Pop lived in their rowhouse. We couldn't find Skipper anywhere, so Dad said we had to turn around and head for home. Maybe he'd show up soon, or the police would look at his collar and bring him home to us safe and sound.

That night I prayed to all the spirits in the Roosevelt Cemetery, asking them to please bring Skipper home to me. I figured that even though I was Catholic and not Jewish like the souls there were, God wouldn't care because he was no particular religion. Why would He care about stupid stuff like that?

We waited for fourteen days and no Skipper, and no call from the Bensalem police. One day when Mom and I were hanging clothes in the small plot of land outside the bar, I started calling Skipper like I always did. Of course, he didn't come running, so I walked out to where I could see the highway with the cars zooming by faster than lightning. I saw something way down the highway, something white with a little black. Could it be Skipper? The colors matched, but there was no way it could be him.

I edged up closer to the side of the highway and looked as far as I could see. Mom called me back to the clothesline, but I needed to find Skipper. If Dad saw me, he would have killed me. No, it couldn't be, but yes, it was Skipper, and I knew he was dead, run over by one of the speeding cars. I ran screaming to Mom. She held me tight, but I couldn't stop crying. I'd lost my best friend. Dad came running from the bar when he heard my godawful screams.

Mom got on the phone right away and asked the township to get Skipper off the highway so we could bury him in our yard. But no one ever came because they said it would be too dangerous for someone to risk their life for a dead dog. Every day we saw Skipper's body lying in the middle of the highway, becoming smaller and smaller, until there was no more Skipper.

Skipper couldn't resist his urge to explore, and I guess that's what happens to all of us when we can't resist doing things we shouldn't be doing. Out wild urges catch up to us and bring us heartbreak. I believe a dog like Skipper didn't deserve it because he didn't understand that actions have consequences. Why did Skipper have to die on the highway like that? Even if there was a reason, I'd never accept it.

Maybe Father Houlihan (we started calling him Father Meatball because he ordered it so much) was right when he said that nothing lasted forever and that we have to learn not to get too attached to the things of the world. I later learned that's a Buddhist philosophy rather than a Catholic one, but I'll take it. That's what you have to do when there are no better answers that make sense.

After Skipper got killed on the Old Lincoln Highway, I never wanted another pet. I couldn't stand the thought of losing one again. Dad and Mom said that if Mom got her dream come true and we moved to a suburban ranch house, we could get a pet if we wanted. It would be able to run free in the neighborhood without being killed on a dangerous highway, but I couldn't think about that now. I wanted Skipper and he was never coming back. Not ever.

Dad did his best to console me in the weeks that followed. We planted a tree in Skipper's memory. I remember how Dad and I bought a dwarf gardenia shrub because Mom loved the smell of gardenias, and so did I. Dad taught me how to dig the dirt and smooth it around the tree. We watered it every day until pretty white flowers bloomed.

Soon, we found new blossoms that eventually turned into beautiful flowers. Skipper would have loved them, but he probably would have eaten them and gotten sick. He was always eating stuff he wasn't supposed to and throwing up. Once we had to take him to the vet who actually gave him medicine to make him throw up after he ate a chocolate bar he found under my bed, or he might have died. Anyway, Dad talked to me about how to plant and take care of the little tree. I felt like Dad and I were the only two people in the universe when we planted that tree, and I wish it could have always been that way with us.

From my time with Suzy Gray/aka Eddie and Skipper, I found out how pets love us unconditionally and how, in their eyes, we can do no wrong. They love us, often more than people do, even when we're grumpy, and we aren't the nicest people in the world. They're there for us when others back away and seem to know when something goes wrong, and we need comfort and understanding with no strings attached.

Losing my pets forced me to think about the uncertainty of life and how things can change in an instant and how you can't count on anything to be the same as it was before. It's all a crap shoot as Mr. Galecki said, and we have to be prepared for whatever comes our way. We can either go with it or give up. If we give up, it will get even worse, trust me. If we go with it and take it as it comes, we'll be granted better times if we choose to live in the present and be grateful for good things that happen.

Planting the tree with Dad showed me that even in the midst of difficult relationships with close family members, we can learn something from the good times we shared, even if they don't happen too often. We can also take time to stage small events with our kids and make memories they'll live with forever, like Dad did from time to time and Mom did all the time.

The words and actions surrounding the planting of that small tree that day with Dad will stay with me forever. Of course, life isn't always so simple. Maybe your parents or other family members let you down completely and you never shared any good moments or very few. In that case, find other people from outside your family who bring you that sense of closeness you deserve. In my life, these moments growing up were few and far between, but they existed, and their memory keeps me going.

Chapter Nine
Teachers I've Known

"Catherine, you are a failure and will always be a failure."
—Sister Margaret Ann to me after my lentil seeds project flopped.

Besides the priests I mentioned in the last chapter, nuns are an important part of my story. They remind me of growing up in the bar because I remember how some of them from my elementary school days would ask my parents to send over some "medicine" (liquor from the bar) when one of the nuns was feeling out of sorts. I wondered how that awful tasting booze could make them feel better. I tried it once when my parents weren't looking and had to spit it out because it tasted disgusting.

I felt sorry for the nuns because they had to teach all day and then share all the household duties like cleaning the bathroom and cooking dinner when they got home at night. They hardly had a free moment to enjoy hobbies, like sewing, needlepoint, or curling up with a good book. I guess because they were women the church thought they didn't count as much as the priests who could change into regular clothes and go out drinking or to a movie with their priest buddies.

The priests even had their own cooks, and even though they served those slimy boiled hot dogs and tasteless meat loaf with canned gravy, they didn't have to think about cooking and cleaning up after themselves like the nuns did. It's a wonder more of them didn't leave the convent, but then they made vows of poverty, chastity, and obedience and took them more seriously than some of the priests did.

I remember all my teachers in Catholic elementary school, but I'll tell about the ones that stood out most. High school was a total disaster until I transferred to public school, so I remember everything about it no matter how much I try to forget it.

I don't remember much about my first-grade teacher, Sister Irene, because Mom and Miss Clara homeschooled me due to my getting every childhood illness ever invented. Sometimes, even enemas didn't help bring down those fevers, as I painfully discovered. The main thing I remember was that Sister Irene congratulated me for passing the test to move on to the next grade when my teachers, Mom and Miss Clara, deserved all the credit for those hours spent studying addition and subtraction and reading those deadly Dick and Jane books. That's when I began to dislike poor Spot, the dog, and his sidekick, Puff, the cat.

By the time I got to third grade they assigned me a lay teacher, one who was not a nun like all the other teachers in Our Lady of Grace School. Her name was Mrs. Blair and she was hell on wheels. For some reason, she took an instant dislike to me, maybe because I was such a brown-noser, and she could see right through me. Being a brown-noser was a pain sometimes, but I wanted people to like me and to think of me as a top student. Also, Dad and Mom loved when I brought home report cards with all A's and comments from my teachers like these: "Your daughter is a pleasure to have in class," or "She is very popular with her classmates and helps them with their schoolwork."

Mrs. Blair couldn't stand me, and one day I gave her a real reason to make her feel that way. Because I was a shy child, I didn't want to ask her for a bathroom pass even though I was ready to burst. She told me to stand up because I'd won a prize in a classroom contest, and all of a sudden, whoosh! I wet myself. A boy in back of me, Paul Parker, started laughing and singing, "Catherine did it, Catherine did it," which clinched it for Mrs. Blair.

She forgot about the award and hustled to my desk with a mop and bucket. "Clean up this mess, young lady. You should be ashamed of yourself."

Paul Parker kept singing how I was the culprit, but the rest of the class remained silent. I never lived it down that I was too shy to ask for a lavatory pass and wet myself instead. Can you believe that I was the same kid who told off Jimmy Porter, that guy at the bar who threatened my father. I must have had a split personality to blast him out and not speak up for myself when I had to pee, or maybe I felt intimidated by the nuns and teachers in Catholic school. I think the class felt sorry for me, everyone except for Paul Parker. From that moment on, I always spoke up for myself, especially when I had to use the bathroom.

Another memorable nun from my early years at OLG was Sister Mary Martha, an elderly sister with a thick Scottish brogue. She lovingly called us *laddies and lassies*, and we did what she asked us because she was a gentle sweet soul, unlike some of the other sisters. She never raised her voice or slapped us with her yardstick or pulled our hair. Out of all the nuns at school, I did my best work for Sister Mary Martha because she loved all of us like our grandmoms did and gave me a reverence and respect for the teaching profession. She was my first role model who led me to become a teacher who tried to put the students' feelings first.

The nun who caused me the most trouble was my seventh-grade nun, Sister Marie Sean, although I loved her name and would have chosen it for myself if I ever decided to become a nun, God forbid. Like many Catholic School girls, I used to put on a veil with bobby pins to hide my hair and string rosary beads around my jeans. Sometimes I'd fashion a white piece that went under the veil with some paper towels to make the habit look more authentic.

I'd run around outside the bar wielding a yard stick to zap the unruly kids in my class. Sometimes, I'd race from one pavement square in back of the bar to another, pretending to be the principal and visit each of the classes, with each stop, filling the class with the fear of God if they'd dared misbehave for Sister Sean Caterina (me!). Power may corrupt, but it sure can be fun being the all-powerful Mother Superior or the sister in charge.

Sister Marie Sean always singled me out because I was a slob when it came to keeping my desk neat. She yelled at me in front of the class and said I was a bad example for everyone because I was a sloppy, bold, brazen article. Don't ask me what that meant, but when a nun wanted to insult a female student, she called her a bold, brazen article.

One year as a teacher I was asked to help evaluate Archbishop Prendergast (Prendy), a Catholic School at the other end of the city. Teachers from the school and evaluators joined each other for lunch each day in the private cafeteria. I innocently asked one of the nuns at the table if they learned the term, *bold, brazen article* when they went to nuns' school. If looks could kill, I'd be a dead duck.

They all glared at me, and didn't speak a word as we ate our Shepherd's pie and Jello. I gulped my food down and got the hell out of there as fast as I could. One of them later confided in me that the sisters felt I could not impartially evaluate their school if I asked that kind of question. Who did I think I was? A couple of the sisters ignored me after my faux-pas in the cafeteria.

My parents met up with Sister Marie Sean in October, our main parents' night of the year. That's the night where your teachers tell your parents secrets about you, they didn't want to know. Sister stood there with her hands on her hips and a scowl on her pimply face when it was Mom and Dad's turn to learn about my performance in her class.

Before Dad and Mom had a chance to shake her hand like they did with the other nuns, Sister, all 90 pounds of her hurled my desk to the floor. My books, tissues, feminine products, and an assortment of movie magazines scattered all over the floor to give testimony to my grunginess. The other parents stopped their conversations to watch Sister Marie Sean blast me out in front of my parents.

"Your daughter is a sloppy mess," Sister told my parents. "She needs to get more organized if she wants to succeed in school and life."

Dad and Mom rolled their eyes and the other parents looked away. Dad said, "Most of her teachers have spoken kindlier about her. Tell us about the problem you have with her."

Mom shot daggers at Sister. "I want you to know we're very proud of her. She wants to become a teacher like you, but I hope she's able to see the good in all her students and not focus on something as trivial as a messy desk like you do."

After that comeuppance, I thought maybe Sister would apologize, but she removed her hands from her hips and crossed her arms. She waited for someone to pick up the desk and all its contents. Happily, no one did, and she was stuck with the job. I ended up getting an A in her class but an unsatisfactory in behavior.

I'll never forget Sister Marie Sean. I can't imagine what her problem was. I guess she didn't understand that some people like me need a messy environment to thrive. My time with her as a teacher reminded me to find something good about every student and let them know how they make the world better in their own way. I remembered it throughout all my years of teaching. I thank my parents for standing by me that day. We stuck together on the important issues, and for that I'm grateful.

After graduating from Our Lady of Grace, some of my friends and I decided to attend High School at Mater Christi (Mother of Christ), a Catholic girls' High School near our neighborhood. They had the weirdest conglomeration of nuns I've ever met. Many of the Sisters came from a far-off country and entered the convent at a school in New York when they were in the ninth grade.

The sisters at Mater Christi's favorite expression was "On the black line, dearies," which they said anytime you deviated from the black row of tiles in the black and white linoleum floors in the hallway. They were insistent that you never stray from the black line lest you incur the wrath of the dour-faced Mother Superior, Mother Agnes Angela. Those floors were so spotless it made you wonder if somebody like Aunt Minnie had spent the day scrubbing them.

One of the Sisters there, Sister Margaret Ann, had as one of her objectives to scar me and some of the other girls for life. I remember one incident in tenth grade where we had to invent and carry out a science project that counted as a major grade. Like a fool, I chose to grow lentil seeds. I should have known it was a bad idea. I'd never met up with a lentil in my life, not even in my parents' restaurant. Mom said she hated them, especially in soup, and the customers didn't want any part of them either.

I watered and fed the lentil seeds for my project, but the little suckers wouldn't grow, and I said so in my report. Looking back, I should have lied and substituted some full-grown lentil plants for the ones that flopped. Sister wasn't hearing any excuses because she believed that every project should end with a positive outcome. Mine ended with droopy lentil leaves and a grade of F in biology for my science project.

The day of our project evaluations, Sister Margaret Ann ordered me to stand up. She stood at my desk and beamed her hawkish eyes at me. "Catherine, you are a failure and will always be a failure, just like your project. I am disappointed in you. Sit down."

If that weren't enough, I started to bawl in front of the whole class and she beat me down more. Could she have been a masochist? Then she called the next student whose project flopped and told her she was and always would be a failure. Of course, the girl started to cry, as I did. Boo hoo, boo hoo, hoo. A bunch of us turned into a sniveling chorus in a Greek tragedy.

You couldn't win with Sister Margaret Ann. She did everything in her power to make you feel hopeless about yourself and your future. When I worked at Girls' High in Philly, I told the students about my science teacher to show them how much things had changed over the years. "Girl, they should see you now. You're a teacher. I guess you showed her, right?"

I smiled and said, "I'm glad I didn't believe what she told me and the others. Sometimes adults don't know everything. That's one thing I know. I hope you do too, and when someone tells you something negative about yourself, consider the source."

Sister Clarita was my favorite nun at Mater Christi. She taught me piano and music at every grade level. She was funny, profane (she loved to use saucy words), and she wore a permanent smile, always building up and encouraging her students. Because of her, I studied piano for many years and developed a lifelong love of all types of music, especially jazz and classical.

At the end of tenth grade, Mom saw how unhappy I was at school and asked if I'd like to switch to public school, the one where Aunt Mary taught. I hugged her and said, "Thanks for understanding that I can't continue at Mater Christi."

Mom hugged me. "I know that going to public school will be a big adjustment, but I believe you'll make it like you do in everything else in life. So, go for it," she said.

My first day at Neshaminy High was a total disaster. My first period English teacher wasn't in the room when I got there. Half the class was standing in the window waiting for her to drive into her parking space and singing, "Here comes Mrs. Hopf in her Hopfomobile." What the heck! The girl in back of me said that Mrs. Hopf was always late to her first class. It turned out that she was the best English teacher I had and made the Romantic poets, like Blake and Wordsworth, come alive for her students. She and Mrs. Henry, my senior teacher at Neshaminy, motivated me to teach English in high school.

I loved how Mrs. Hopf wore wild polka dotted dresses in yellow and black with red costume jewelry and used unconventional methods, like lively debates and class discussions, to teach her class. She always encouraged us to speak our minds, even back then when people didn't usually buck the system by using fresh, new teaching methods like debates and discussions, instead of diagramming sentences and giving multiple-choice quizzes.

The other thing that happened the first day I was there involved Stan Weismann, who later became my best platonic male friend. He started messing around in Mrs. Hopf's class and calling out dumb stuff as he always did because he was the class clown. Mrs. Hopf would not tolerate acting out in class, so she grabbed him by the ear and dragged him to the principal's office for disrupting her class.

The principal told Stan to report to his office during her class period for the next month and to bring his work. Stan wasn't happy about that, but it saved Mrs. Hopf some grief for a few weeks. Despite his antics, Stan had a good heart and went out of his way to help people, like the day he woke up at six AM and walked from Levittown (five miles away) to shovel our driveway so Dad could get to work on time. Dad and Mom never forgot his kindness.

Another stellar teacher at Neshaminy was Mrs. Henry, a proper lady with a sweet Southern draw, who taught senior English. One day we had to give oral book reports and Harvey Green flashed his red book cover to the rows of kids sitting before him. After he gave his report, Mrs. Henry asked with all the excellent classic books in the world why Harvey chose Salinger's *The Cather in the Rye* for his book report.

"I loved the book," Harvey said, "and I think my classmates will love it too. Salinger said exactly what it was like to be a teenager in our generation and for generations to come. I'm glad I chose this book and hope everyone wants to read it after I give them a taste of it. And no, I'm not sorry I did it, Mrs. Henry."

The class cheered and Harvey went back to his desk. Mrs. Henry gave him a small smile. "You gave an interesting report, but I hope that when your classmates choose a book, they'll pick something more appropriate without all those curse words and gloomy thoughts."

Mrs. Henry's words only made us want to read the book more. In fact, that very day, I drove to the bookstore and picked up a copy as did many of my classmates, who couldn't wait to get their hands on it. I lay in bed that night, wanting to stay awake to finish the book, that's how much I loved it. When I became a teacher, it was one of my favorite books to teach, and the kids asked to read more books like it. The book turned more kids on to reading than most of the books on the required American literature reading list.

Did Mrs. Henry know something about motivating kids to read that we kids didn't? Was she using reverse psychology, or was she an old fuddy-duddy and party pooper who didn't want kids to see the world as it really was? Maybe she was a precursor of the book banners who would appear during the reign of reactionary politicians. All I know is that whatever she said that day worked.

Mom also read the book and had nothing but praise for it. When she read the part about Holden trying to erase the F-word from the wall of his sister's school, "That young man in the book was a saint at heart. He wanted to save the children" Here's the passage from the book that Mom and I discussed:

"That's the whole trouble," I said. "You can't ever find a place that's nice and peaceful, because there aren't any. You may think there is, but once you get there, when you're not looking, somebody'll sneak up and write, 'Fuck you' right under your nose."

In her own way, Mrs. Henry taught us not to shy away from controversy and from motivating students to speak their truth about literature and life and to read anything we like. To take that away from them deprives them of thinking freely. What do you think?

Chapter Ten
505 Azalea Lane

"Making this move will be the first step to a new life for all of us."
—Mom to Dad about moving from the Royal Gardens

When I reached double digits, Mom saw a picture in the local paper of a three-bedroom, one-bath, stone front ranch house in Langhorne with teal shutters that a local builder was offering. She loved the house on 505 Azalea Lane from the first day she saw a picture of it *The Bucks County Courier Times*. "This is my dream house, "she told me. "We're going to live there one day, but I need to prepare your father first, so don't say anything."

"You can count on me, Mom. I'm in," I said, hugging her. I shouted out Uncle Tony's famous words, "Yippy Kay Yay, the one that cowboys used to say," and added his magic word, Relsteen, with the accent on the second syllable, for good measure.

I couldn't imagine having our own home blanketed by an acre of velvety green lawn, maple trees, and flowers in every color of the rainbow. Everything was in full bloom in the ad, like people had lived there for years and it had just sprung up from out of nowhere. Plus, Mom said she loved planting flowers. She didn't care about touching squiggly, slimy worms and couldn't wait to see the flowers in all her favorite colors of red, pink, and purple, along with golden daffodils with their sweet subtle scent, lining the paved path to our new house.

My whole life, I lived on top of a bar where a sign that went *whee whoo* kept me awake half the night, and I talked to the spirits of dead people in the Roosevelt Cemetery, but I don't mean to complain. Who else got to have friends like Miss Laura, Miss Clara, and the guys at the bar, like Doctor Alex, Mr. Cuff, and Mr. Galecki, who were way more interesting than the people my friends who lived in the suburbs hung out with.

To me, 505 was a mystical number because it meant angel communication, and I always talked to the angels when I prayed. I found out some interesting stuff about angel numbers in books I got out of the library (the local one, not the school one, because nuns said it was a mortal sin to study secret angel numbers because it was against the first commandment. Just about everything was a mortal sin to them.)

I always wondered why religion couldn't be fun and upbeat. Most of the stuff they preached at school and church was gloom and doom. I didn't consider psychic stuff sinful. After all, Jesus turned water to wine at the wedding feast at Cana, gave sight back to the blind man, and brought Lazarus back from the dead. If He made miracles and did superhuman things, it couldn't be a sin, right?

I also learned that the magical number 505 meant that better days were coming, a saying Mom always used, especially with Dad, when he was about to give up hope, which was fairly often because of his bipolar disorder.

"Better days are coming, Emidio," she'd say. He'd shake his head, purse his lips and scrunch his eyebrows. "Yeah, Grace? I'd like to know when. Tell me when."

"Think about it, Emidio. Making this move to the new house will be the first step to a new life for all of us. Trust me." Gradually, she wore him down, and in the end, he talked like he liked the idea of moving. I wasn't surprised to learn that the street number of the ranch house Mom loved also meant the ability to expand your curiosity and the world around you. Mom loved it when I told her that the house numbers had a secret meaning. Every time she mentioned her dream house to Dad, she'd smile and say, "Better days are coming," like a mantra, until he began to believe it. Talk about magic!

After running the bar for over thirty years with Dad, Mom somehow convinced him that we should close down the business and move to the house in Azalea Lane, Bucks County. Dad said he wasn't ready to retire but that he needed more space and would love to have his own plot of ground to garden, where he could do what he enjoyed best, away from the bar and his insane work schedule.

Even though Dad acted like he wanted to move, my parents went back and forth over whether to buy the house and had some pretty loud arguments over it. Dad worried that he wouldn't be able to run the restaurant without Mom, who had set her heart on retiring. One of Dad's customers, Ryan, offered to help him make sandwiches and heat up soups he'd buy from a supplier, one who would never put his spoon back in sauce or soup after he licked it, like Fred the Cook and the other chefs at The Royal Gardens did. Dad was okay with Ryan helping out, but he still dreaded running the business without Mom making all the major decisions and deal with the finances.

One day when Dad was in an unusually good mood, Mom and Dad decided to take the plunge and buy the ranch house. The plan was that dad would keep working a few more years and then get a part-time job, tend his garden, and go out drinking with his buddies from the bar, but Mom said we'll see about that part.

Mom got pissed whenever Dad mentioned going out with his friends because of all the nights we were left alone with her radio shows and the fact that Dad once cheated on her. Dad tried to calm Mom down by saying that after he stopped working at the bar, he'd get a part-time job at a local eatery, doing what he knew best, tending bar and short-order cooking. This time he left out the part about drinking with his buddies and getting into trouble with wild ladies like Ada.

Dad couldn't take the stress of thinking about the many changes coming his way if we moved, so he decided to increase his visits to the psychiatrist, who still loved to talk about his sex life with Mom. Of course, that weirded her out, and she stopped going to the sessions with him. Dad's doctors gave him more powerful psychotropic drugs, and he calmed down but acted more zombified, to the point where nothing rattled him, even the prospect of moving to 505 Azalea Lane. This made Mom reconsider and start going to the doctor with him again. Dad being a zombie wasn't an option for her.

"I'll be okay," he said, "I'm going to be my old self again. You wait and see." but I wondered if he believed it.

After Dad bribed his friends at the bar with free beer, they helped us pack our stuff in cardboard boxes we got from the liquor store, and presto, chango, we were on our way to starting our new lives. Miss Laura stayed on to clean for the new owners, but I'm sure she still complained about the smelly pee on the bathroom floor.

Miss Laura told Dad she was sorry about threatening to leave because of the disgusting bathrooms and work for the Holiday Inn down the road. She said she could never have done that, no matter how much those guys peed on her clean floor, because my dad and mom were like family. But the whole time she worked at the Royal Gardens she was in charge, and we all knew it, especially Dad.

Miss Clara moved on to the diner down the road when the restaurant closed. She told me how she missed teaching me catechism even though she thought a lot of the rules in the Catholic Church we talked about were dumb, like not eating meat on Friday or telling our sins in confession to another person, who happened to be a priest who didn't know much about life because he hadn't experienced it.

She didn't tell me she felt that way until I was in high school, because she didn't want to rile up my parents. According to her, the non-denominational church she left wasn't much better. She said she's still shopping for a new religion and doesn't know if she'll find one that doesn't make her feel like she'll burn in hell forever after she dies.

When we moved to our new home, I enjoyed taking the school bus to Our Lady of Grace School. Dad didn't have to drive me when we lived in no man's land on the Superhighway because they didn't have bus service in no-man's land. I could even invite friends over to our house now that we didn't live on the most dangerous highway in the world.

I knew I'd love our home on Azalea Lane because I had my very own yellow room where I didn't hear the Royal Gardens sign blowing back and forth in the wind, but I kind of missed the spirits in the Roosevelt Cemetery calling out to me and waking me out of a sound sleep. I hoped they'd come back some day with their comforting words and predictions, or I'd have to learn to depend on my deepening psychic superpowers to teach me about life, death, and ever after.

Even if I never improved those super powers or talked to the dead souls, I felt happy we moved into our own home, far, far, from the restaurant and bar, where I could play tag with my friends in our huge yard or lie in a lounge chair with my favorite book, and have cookouts every weekend. Best of all, I wouldn't have to disappear when Dad's friends at the bar talked men talk or Mom was busy cooking big dinners or the Kiwanis Club and didn't want me to pester her about trivia like getting me my own bra and girdle, and having to tell Aunt Minnie to carry me piggy back to the farm to shut me up.

After my parents decided to buy the ranch house, the builders got to work right away and put the finishing touches on it so we could move in the spring, just six months away. We ordered flowering bushes and a pink dogwood tree from the nursery and Mom's favorite, a deep pink crabapple tree.

My favorite room in our new house was the family room, where I'd listen to Ahmed Jamal records with my friends and watch Bandstand when I became a teenager. Every day, I looked forward to tying a jump rope around a doorknob and pretending I was dancing like the Bandstand regulars, Justine and Bob, or Arlene and Kenny. They were like celebrities with their own fan clubs and magazine articles. Dick Clark, the man who hosted a New Year's Eve show for years, ran Bandstand, which started in Philly and turned into a national show.

The kitchen at Azalea Lane had red Formica countertops and the latest new appliances for Mom to show off her cooking skills, this time for our own family. She decorated the family room in shades of burnt toast and gold. A fireplace flickered all winter, warming our culos and our souls. Mom often made hot chocolate and butter cookies for my friends who visited after school to watch Bandstand and play board games. They all loved Mom and said they wish their moms were more like her.

Chapter Eleven
Friends I've Known

"If you ever pull a stunt like that again, you will be expelled."
—the principal to me and my friends

Once we moved to Azalea Lane, I started to invite friends over from school. My friends' parents gained new respect for us because we moved from a restaurant and bar to an actual ranch house with a huge landscaped yard. The dangerous superhighway where the restaurant was located made it a scary place for kids and parents alike.

To drive along that highway where cars raced by at top speed posed a hazard, and once kids were dropped off there, their parents told Mom and Dad they worried that their kids would come in contact with drunks and miscreants and God knows who else. Maybe Dad would be willing to drop me off at their house for playdates. The only problem was that Dad worked day and night and didn't have time. So, for the first few years of my life, the people who stopped at the Royal Gardens for drinks were my main friends.

The first good friend I met when I moved to Azalea Lane was Aliz Kobok, who lived on the other side of the Lincoln Highway. Her parents were Hungarians, but my friend didn't speak her native language and fully embraced the American culture, which troubled her parents because she acted more like an American teenager than most of her peers did. Aliza's dad was protective of her and watched her every move.

When we walked uptown to Langhorne to get our cherry cokes and Tastykakes at the drugstore, he followed two paces behind us with a blazing flashlight and smoked a cigar while he waited for us outside. After reading every teen magazine on the rack, gulping down our cherry cokes and licking our ice cream cones, we made the trip home in the darkness with Mr. Kobok and his trusty flashlight following us.

Aliz's mother always offered us our favorite snacks and made me feel at home whenever I visited. One day Aliz told me that her mom was embarrassed because her house wasn't fully furnished. I told her I didn't care since I lived on top of the bar for the first few years of my life, and our apartment was sparsely furnished because my parents didn't have time to think about it because they were too busy building the business. To this day, fancy furnishings mean nothing to me. The people who live in the house are more important to me than leather chairs or plush carpets. On second thought, I guess a little of both mindsets would be good.

One afternoon, Alize told me her mom was cooking goulash and wanted me to join the family for dinner. I had an irrational fear of trying new foods; I'd never tried goulash and didn't relish the prospect of eating something I'd never eaten before. Alize had joined our family for lasagna or chicken marsala many times, but she was more adventurous and didn't have qualms about trying something new. In fact, she looked forward to it and always liked whatever Mom served. Out of all my grade school friends, Mom loved Alize best. She called Mom "Mrs. Emidio," and my mom always mentioned how Alize was the perfect child, besides me, of course.

I told Alize that I was sorry I couldn't make it for dinner because I had to help Mom clean the house. I usually didn't like to lie, and this was a big one because I hated cleaning and
always made myself scarce on cleaning days although Mom was quick to catch on. I was sorry I didn't go to my friend's house to eat goulash that night and even sorrier that I'd lied. But the fear of divine retribution was not as bad as trying a new food. What would I do if I didn't like it? Spitting it out was out of the question as I didn't want Aliz and her family to think I was a slob, and they didn't have a dog that I could sneak it to under the table.

The next time Alize asked me to eat at her house, my guilt caught up with me, and I accepted. Her mom made stuffed peppers, and I always hated peppers in any way, shape, or form, but I enjoyed eating the ones Mrs. Kobok made and made sure to let her know. She invited me again the following week and I didn't even ask what she was cooking. I knew it would be good.

Alize moved to Arizona when her dad developed breathing problems. She returned to Bucks County, PA, occasionally, and we got together. Years later we met up on Facebook and had a brief falling out over politics. I missed her and felt sad that we'd grown apart, and we both decided we shouldn't let politics stand in the way of a lifelong friendship.

Mom always said that there are more important things to think about than political differences and that friendship should always win out, and that's exactly what happened when we agreed not to discuss that subject again on Facebook or anywhere. I can't wait to see Aliza again. She usually comes back to Pennsylvania once a year and we meet, along with some other friends, at a restaurant to catch up.

My best friend from school, Dorcy, whom I met in second grade, lived in a Cape Cod a few miles away from me. Her dad was a carpenter, whose workshop bordered the property. Once, when we were playing in the workshop, I ripped open my leg on one of the tools, and her parents tried to patch it up themselves. Dad and Mom were angry that Darcy's parents didn't call them or take me to the hospital. It left a big scar, but I learned the hard way never to go near dangerous tools again. Dorcy's dad was the only parent who would pick me up and drive me to their house, but he drove down the Superhighway like an absolute maniac, and I feared for my life and Dorcy's.

Dorcy wasn't afraid of her Dad's driving, but I closed my eyes and said "Hail Mary's" the whole way to their bungalow, and when we got there I let out a big "Phew," which made her dad say, "What's wrong, Cassie? I thought you liked amusement park rides." I swear her dad was crazy even though he was kind enough to give me rides to their house and stop for ham hoagies at Casa Di Pizza along the way.

Dorcy's Mom always wore tight pants and a form-fitting top. She wasn't pretty but made the most of her looks. Once for a joke, she made us makeshift bras out of bathing suit tops, like Mom did for me at the bar when I screamed for a brassiere and a girdle. Dorcy's mom took it a step farther by sticking carrot tops in the "bras" to fill them out. Even though we tried to be good Catholic girls, we enjoyed showing off our new bosoms since our real ones hadn't grown in yet. I couldn't wait to stop being "a skinny crab," the awful name a few of the boys called me when they saw me in a two-piece bathing suit at the local pool. I rarely went to the pool after that, and if I did, I wore jeans and a T-shirt.

Dorcy and I remained good friends until eleventh grade. When she found out I'd transferred to public high school, she predicted I'd lose my religion. She graduated from Mater Christi High School and went on to marry and have two daughters. Years later, we had a grade school reunion where we hugged and made a fuss over one another. A few years after the reunion, when she was in her early forties, Dorcy died of breast cancer, leaving her husband with two pre-teen daughters to raise. I felt that I had lost a part of my childhood.

Other friends from grade school and high school included Mary Ellen, Marcy, and Darlene. We hung out every day after school when we didn't have tons of homework. We loved walking to the center of Langhorne to the Langhorne drugstore to get cherry cokes and Philly's famous TastyKakes, like Butterscotch Krimpets and chocolate cupcakes with cream in the middle. We used to have sleepovers monthly: we called them pajama parties when we were kids. Our moms set up cots in the basement where we could blast our Fats Domino and Little Richard records as loudly as we wanted. Once, my buddies gathered me up in a big blanket and threatened to tickle me to death. They knew how ticklish I was, and the other girls didn't mind it as much, so I became the ideal candidate for tickling.

I begged them to stop, but they wouldn't, and no one heard my screams. I guess Mom thought we were having fun, so she didn't check to see what was happening. I didn't realize at the time that tickling was a form of torture, but after they got done tickling me, I knew it for sure. It's crazy the stuff kids do to one another in the name of fun. I shrugged it off and things were fine between me and my buddies until ninth grade at Mater Christi.

My friends knew how scared I was of mice after I told them we found a couple in our laundry room at Azalea Lane. After I saw their tiny corpses, I couldn't sleep in my room unless I pushed towels up against my door to fill up all the empty space so Minnie and Mickey couldn't get in. Mom called the same exterminator we had at the Royal Gardens, and he sprayed his foul-smelling potion in every room.

I still slept with the light on for fear one of the critters would nibble my toes in the middle of the night. I was more afraid of mice than I was of death, and that's no lie. Finally, the mice disappeared, and I could sleep again. The exterminator reminded me how mice got stuck in one of Raymond's (his client's hair) and they took up residence there. He reassured me that the mice had left our house at Azalea Lane and that there was nothing to fear. Thank God it turned out to be true.

Mice surfaced again in my sophomore year of high school, but it didn't end up ok this time. My three good friends, Maryellen, Marcy, and Darlene and I rode the school bus together every day and sat together. One spring day on the ride home, Maryellen brought out a cage she'd hidden on the floor with her rain jacket. Yikes! She opened the door and four mice fell out, dropping on to my lap and dancing around me and chirping like madmen.

What could I do but scream like Janet Lee in "Psycho." This set off a chain reaction. The bus driver stopped the bus, pulled into a rest area, and told us to behave until she got back to the bus. She was hopping mad. I could tell because I heard her cursing. I think she said every curse word I ever heard at the bar, including the b-word and the f-word.

She came back and told us she'd called the principal, Mother Agnes Angela, from the phone inside the restaurant and that she was mortified that such chaos would break out on the bus. Mother Agnes said there would be severe consequences.

We rode back to school in total silence. The mice rode up front with the bus driver, where she kept a watchful eye on them so they wouldn't escape from their cage. Mother Agnes was waiting at the door for us when we arrived at school. She gave us one of her menacing looks; her eyebags were puffy and dark, and she looked like Bela Lugosi, who played Count Dracula in the horror movie. She told us to wait for her in her office. We waited while she rang the bell for the next period; we waited while she said morning prayers over the PA. We waited until she decided to mete out our punishment.

Mother Agnes breathed a long sigh, sat at her desk, and crossed her arms. "Ladies, you caused a terrible commotion on the bus. The driver said she could not concentrate on her driving. She could have gotten into a tragic accident because of you. Since you were the one who screamed the loudest, Catherine, what do you have to say for yourself?"

"I couldn't help acting that way, Mother Agnes. Now I wish I hadn't because I know that what I did was wrong, and I'm sorry."

She looked at the other three girls. "What possessed you to let those mice loose when you knew how afraid your friend was of rodents?"

Since Maryellen was the one who let the mice out of the cage, she answered. "I thought it would be funny to tease our friend and see how she reacted. I never thought she'd act so crazy because of mice. If I had, I'd never have let the mice loose. It was all my idea, so don't blame the others, Mother."

Mother Agnes frowned. "Yes, but they went along with the prank, didn't you, girls?"

No one said anything, but Mother didn't miss a beat. She got up from her swivel chair and looked at the picture of Mother Mary that hung in her office. The Blessed Mother wore a white cape and blue veil and smiled like she loved us with all her heart despite the fact that my friends teased me, and I screamed like a maniac and my friends caused it.

Mother Agnes stood looking at Mother Mary's picture, then turned to us. "As Mater Christi students, you are always supposed to follow Mother Mary's example and act like perfect ladies in all situations. After all, our school is named after her."

We sat there dumbfounded and wondered what would happen next. Would we be suspended, or even worse, expelled from Mater Christi? What would our parents say if we disgraced them that way?

Mother Agnes went back to her desk and wrote something in her notebook. She stared at us for a long moment. "Girls, I'm going to suspend all of you for three days. Pick up your assignments from your teachers before you leave the building today. You'll also each write a letter to the bus driver apologizing for your misbehavior. If you ever pull a stunt like this again, you will be expelled instantly. I'll be watching all of you carefully to be sure you deserve to be called Mater Christi girls. Don't disappoint me."

The principal signaled for us to leave. I couldn't get out of there soon enough. My friends and I didn't speak on the way back to our classes. I felt betrayed by them and didn't think that I deserved the same punishment since they initiated the incident. I didn't speak to them for a long time after that. In retrospect, I believe I deserved the same penalty since I disrupted things as much as I did. After we resumed our friendship, they didn't pull any more pranks, and I didn't react as strongly to their shenanigans.

Sharon was another friend during my high school years. The Morrisey's lived around the corner from Azalea Lane. Sharon and I walked to each other's house every day to play board games after school and trekked to the drugstore to sit on stools and eat snacks. Sharon's dad, Dr. Morrisey, worked from his home as a family doctor. Doctor Morrisey was a gentle, quiet guy who played La Vie en Rose on the organ and walked with a limp from a childhood bout with Polio.

I was shocked to find out that his wife, my friend Sharon's mom, was a mean, hateful woman. She also suffered from alcoholism. A few times Mom sent me to her house with the same medicine she'd sent the nuns, but her preference was bourbon or scotch rather than a tamer liquor. When she got drunk, she became mean and abusive. Once she threatened to annihilate her husband. She was a nurse in her husband's office and knew her stuff better than any medical person I've met; however, at home, she made life hell for her husband and kids.

Her son, Jonah, was a homely young man, a little older than his sister Sharon. I hated how Mrs. Morrisey forced us to take him everywhere: our trips to the drugstore, the playground, and especially, Church, where he nodded his head a hundred times every time the priest said the holy name of Jesus. I know you're supposed to bow your head when Jesus is mentioned, but I thought his head would roll off because he did it so many times. I heard he wanted to study for the priesthood. He was about seven feet tall and was so thin that a strong wind could blow him into oblivion. He had flaming red hair that stuck up like Alfalfa from the "Our Gang Comedy" show.

I was embarrassed to be seen with him. Boys seemed to avoid both my friend Sharon and me whenever Jonah accompanied us anywhere, but if we dared leave the house without him, Mrs. Morrisey would peek around the corner and say, "What about Jonah? Doesn't he deserve to have fun too?" and we were stuck with him.

Mom always encouraged us to treat Jonah kindly because he had a rough life at home with his parents who had a totally dysfunctional marriage, as far as I could see. I became an expert on that after living with Mom and Dad all those years. I was glad I didn't have to lug around my brother everywhere I went. He had his own friends and sports to keep him busy. Jonah was just plain weird, if you asked me, but I learned something about how painful excluding kids can be to the person no one wants to befriend.

Strangely, he grew up to be a good-looking guy, put on a few pounds, and ended up becoming a doctor like his father. I heard that he still nodded whenever he heard Jesus' name in church or when someone said it in vain, but hey, everyone has their own relsteens as Uncle Tony used to say. I think as long as they don't hurt anyone by doing that, it's perfectly okay.

Sharon decided to enter the Sisters of Mercy after high school. She'd dreamed all her life of becoming a nurse like her mom, but the religious order had different plans for her. She became an elementary teacher, which was a shame because she never liked math or reading, and working with little kids wasn't her thing. Meek, quiet girl that she was, Sharon conceded to what was best for her religious order and she learned to enjoy her job teaching in a Catholic grade school. The pastor even promoted her to assistant principal.

A few years later, I caught up with her and found out that she'd left the convent. They told her that she had to go back home to her house near Azalea Lane and care for her mother who was suffering from the mental and physical effects of alcoholism. According to her superiors, her first obligation was to her mother. Her father, Dr. Morrisey, had long since died of a heart attack, probably from the stress he suffered at the hands of his wife.

Sharon and I went our separate ways and lost touch over the years. One day I called her. I'd heard that she lived in Yardley, around the corner from me, and had worked as an elementary school teacher in a Catholic grade school. The principal of her school gave me Sharon's phone number, and I called her and asked how she had been doing since she left the Sisters of Mercy. She said she met a man, one of her student's widowed fathers, and they had a short, whirlwind courtship before marrying. She had one baby, a daughter, Daniella, named after her dad, Daniel, whom she adored.

She said that everything was fine in her life, except that on the nights when she was fertile, she'd have to lie in her bed reciting the rosary so she wouldn't give into her baser instincts and commit a mortal sin by using birth control. Yikes! Did she actually believe that God would strike her dead if she didn't conceive a baby every time she had sex?

I never heard from Sharon again after that. When I told Mom about our conversation, she laughed. "Why do people torture themselves like that? Why don't they use their common sense?" I figured institutions like home, church, and school, have more power over us than we think and sometimes cause us to go against our better judgment.

My friend, Carol, whom I met at Neshaminy High school, helped me adjust to public school after attending Catholic school for umpteen years; she is the friend I keep in contact with to this day. We feel free to say anything that's on our minds to each other and do not take offense, no matter how strongly we differ in our opinions. We saw each other through happy times, like having our babies; personal achievements, like graduating from college and landing our first jobs as teachers; to sad times, like losing our parents.

Carol is a lot like Mom because she listens when you talk like no one else in the world, and she gives great advice. Like Mom, she's always there when you need her. My mom loved it when she visited us in Azalea Lane. Her face always lit up when she saw Carol, and vice versa. We experienced many of life's passages together, like high school, and now that we're grandmothers, we look forward to being friends forever after.

Marsha, whom I met while teaching in Philly, also remains one of my dearest friends. We love the same books and movies and share the same life philosophy. We commiserate about growing older, about medical issues, and what the future will bring. Deep down, we're still English teachers who love *The Great Gatsby* and watch re-runs of "Splendor in the Grass," a la William Wordsworth, the Romantic poet.

What do friends mean in your life? Why are they important? I know they help me think about who I am, what I stand for, and where I'm moving toward in the future.

Chapter Twelve
From Head Honcho to Peon

"She looks dead. How can she look good?
—me, upon hearing somebody comment on a family member's dead
body

Dad continued working at the bar until the crazy hours got to be too much for him. By this time, a bunch of new customers started coming around every day in sleeveless undershirts in the dead of winter with their underarm hair sticking out, sporting raunchy, colorful tattoos. "Yo, Joe," they'd say, holding up their mugs to him, "Fill 'er up, and make it pronto." The days of Mr. Cuff, Mr. Galecki, and a bunch of other customers who never gave him agita and always had Dad's back were long gone. At least Dad could reason with them and tell them it was time to leave if they insisted on more or stronger drinks.

These new customers often showed their rowdiness to the point that Dad couldn't handle them by appealing to their common sense, because they had none, according to him. Some of his substitute bartenders, guys he thought were his friends, began to offer free beers to everyone at Dad's u-shaped bar when they took over for him. Dad quickly put a stop to that when he asked one of his old friends, Murph, to watch the bar when he wasn't there. Sure enough, Dad was right, so he fired his sorry stand-ins and asked his friend Murph to stand watch on a regular basis, which he did. Those hooligans never robbed him again.

Dad found it hard to keep up with his new, more hectic schedule. Without Mom around to bounce things off of and with some of his new customers he nicknamed "The Derries," short for *derelicts*, he didn't enjoy his work like he used to. He was sixty-two and felt that he was too young to retire, but he started talking to Pop about selling the business and the farm. That way, my grandfather could live out his final years in his row house in peace in northeast Philly with Aunt Minnie and Uncle Tony, sitting on the couch down the basement next to Nan, listening to "The Italian Hour" with a bottle of beer in his hand.

My grandparents insisted on complete silence, which was sometimes a challenge for Uncle Tony and Aunt Minnie who loved to pick on one another, especially when "The Italian Hour," which started in the 50s, played my grandparents favorite Italian songs in their native and new language.

"Che La Luna" featured bawdy lyrics, but my grandparents took it in stride and stomped their feet and clapped their hands when songs like this played. They laughed at the lyrics and didn't make a big deal like some holier-than-thou fools who get all prissy when they hear raunchy lyrics. My grandparents mainly loved the opera songs they played, like "O mio Babbino Carro" and "La Donna e Mobile," which made them tear up, along with me, who loved the melodies but didn't understand most of the lyrics.

After a particularly hard day, I heard Dad tell Mom that he was ready to retire from The Royal Gardens. Aldo, a local restaurant and bar owner he was friends with, told Dad that when he was ready to retire to let him know. Also, he'd love to have him come work for him as a bartender and short-order cook. The Bucks County Lounge was down the road from our house on Azalea Lane, and Dad liked the way Aldo ran the business. Aldo had a peaceful clientele, unlike some of the rabble rousers that made up most of his current customers at The Royal Gardens.

That year, right after Christmas, Dad started his new job at The Bucks County Lounge in Langhorne, Bucks County, as Joe the Bartender. He liked to say he went from "Head Honcho" to "Peon." Some of his older, tamer customers that he'd known for years followed him there once The Royal Gardens closed down. The Lounge offered rooms for rent and had a full-time chef, who cooked Italian specialties like Chicken Cacciatore and Shrimp Scampi, so the patrons brought their wives and made it a weekend getaway. They even had karaoke, where people could win prizes for their singing. Did Aldo know Dad better than he knew himself? It seemed that way to me.

Many of Dad's geezer friends revived their romantic days at the lounge. The only bad thing about it was that they had to share a bathroom with the other guests staying there. Dad used to laugh about that because he couldn't stand sharing his bathroom with Mom, Joe, and me. He never cleaned the tub when he took a bath or shower, and Joe and I used to get into big arguments about it with him.

We couldn't stand the gray, scummy ring Dad left around the tub or the soapy mess in the shower, along with a pool of water on the floor. All he'd say to Joe and me was "You guys can move out if you don't like it. It can't be soon enough," and we'd shut up for fear he'd lock us out of the house one day if one of his gloomy moods took over. He could change from Dr. Jekyl to Mr. Hyde in a millisecond. Dad could never stand criticism unless he was dishing it out. He thought he was always right.

When you stayed overnight at The Bucks County Lounge, you had to put on a frowsy bathrobe that the hotel provided and schlep to the bathroom with your butt hanging out. Seeing all those people with big stomachs and butts parading around would have grossed me out.

A few months after we moved into our new house, Mrs. Kenderdine, the lady next door, had this gigantic beagle dog who had a litter of puppies. She offered one to Mom, who gladly accepted. Dad wasn't crazy about dogs since we had Skipper and he died on the highway, but he thought it would be fun to have a pet again. Mom thought it might encourage Dad to start exercising by walking the dog, which he needed, since his doctor told him it would help his depression.

My brother got so excited thinking about getting the puppy that he did a dance and whooped like crazy. The dog was a chocolate color, mostly beagle with a fierce beagle bark. Mom liked the name Maxey, short for Maximillian, Archduke of Austria. She read about him in her history class at Eastern High School and thought it was a powerful name.

My brother Joe liked the name, and he wanted to add "Good Doggie" to the dog's name, so it became "Maxey, Good Doggie (with the accent on the second syllable of *doggie*)." To us, Maxey was the best dog in the world, and that's why Mom and I agreed on adding, "Maxey, Good Doogie," the second part to his name. That was a mouthful to say, but Mom, Joe, and I thought our wonder-pup deserved a fancy name. Dad said it was ridiculous for a dog to have two names and told us just to call him Maxey. Naturally, we didn't listen.

Maxey came running when you called him either name, "Maxie" or "Good Doggie," but he went wild when you called him "Maxie, Good Doggie." The first thing he'd do was jump up on all fours until he almost knocked you over (sometimes he did) and slobber all over you. Dad hated him when he did that, but Maxie Good Doggie never listened to anything Dad said. Dad cursed him out a few times, even saying the "*F*-word," but it never did any good. Maxie jumped and slobbered on him a thousand times more.

Maxey practically knocked everyone over and drooled on everyone, especially delivery and repair people; most people hated it, but Dad loved to watch them call him off and didn't lift a finger to save them from Maxey's spirited greetings.

Maxey lived for quite a few years. One day he got loose and ran straight to the Superhighway, the same one where Skipper, my first dog, got run over. Maxey died the exact same way that Skipper did. Only this time, someone from the township came to remove him. We never got another dog after that.

A couple of years after Pop Pop sold The Royal Gardens, he had a stroke, but he was still able to sit on the couch next to Nan Nan, the love of his life. They'd watch TV all day and visit with their kids and grandkids.

In her eighties and nineties, Nan Nan continued to run up and down the steep basement steps to the kitchen make our family's favorite foods, like spaghetti and meatballs with a side of braciola (flank steak rolled up with cheeses and spices) smothered in Nan Nan's thick tomato gravy, which were both loaded with garlic. Pop Pop would slice giant loaves of Italian bread and sharp provolone that hung from the basement ceiling to ripen. He'd hold the bread and cheese so close to his chest when he sliced them, and I thought he might cut his heart out. Thank God he never did.

My grandparents ate big lunches (they always had dinner for lunch): salad with fresh olives, provolone, tomato and basil sandwiches, and sometimes spaghetti sauce made with fresh tomatoes that Nan Nan canned in the summer to savor on cold winter days. Every Sunday at noon, Mom, Dad, their kids and grandkids would visit and polish off big plates of macaroni, meatballs, and braciola. Usually, Uncle Louie, Dad's brother would come with his wife and two daughters who had beautiful voices and sang "Send in the Clowns."

After a while, Pop Pop's heart gave out and he died, but I didn't attend his funeral. When I was fourteen, my grandmother Carmella, on my mom's side, died, and her family had a viewing for her at the Leonard J. Ruck Funeral Home in Baltimore. After that, I vowed never to attend another funeral if there was a dead body present.

I couldn't stand seeing Grandmother laid out in a chiffon pink gown, all made up with orangey pink lipstick and coral blush. She never wore much make-up when she was alive, so why should she wear it when she died? At 62, her hair didn't have any gray in it, and it was short and wavy like mine is today.

She always called me Catherine Louise and once gave me a big, fancy princess doll with a sparkling tiara for Christmas. Another Christmas she gave me a gold music box that played Ave Maria. I remember going to her beautiful house on Old Harford Road in Baltimore for holiday celebrations, which a ton of people attended. People would dance and old Mr. Mike (Signore Michele), a neighbor, would play the kazoo.

Grandmother used to rent out some of the rooms in her house to boarders who had just come to America looking for a new, prosperous life. One young couple, Sven and Elsa, showed us how they'd decorated their Christmas tree with paper flags as ornaments in the Swedish tradition. Grandmother helped them achieve their dream of coming to America to discover freedom and prosperity.

A couple of years before she died, when I was twelve, Mom and I visited Grandmother at her home in Baltimore in our blue and white mother-daughter dresses adorned with sassy blue French poodles. I was anything but cute when I talked back to Mom that day. We'd taken the train and had eaten in the dining car, which was great fun for both of us. They served strawberry shortcake slathered with whipped cream for dessert.

When we'd gotten out of the cab to Grandmother's house, I was rude to Mom for no reason. Like many kids that age with raging hormones, I showed her how mouthy and brazen I could be. I told Mom to shut up and said that I hated her. By the time we arrived at Grandmother's, Mom was ready to slap my face, as parents often did in those days when kids acted out. No one would think of reporting them to the police because they were only exercising their parental rights, and they believed the kid deserved it.

Grandmother witnessed the whole ugly scene and said to Mom, "Don't you hit that child," but, in the next breath, she said to me, "Catherine Louise, come back and see me when you're sweet sixteen. Never talk to your mother like that again," I immediately apologized to Mom and Grandmother. I didn't know where my nasty words came from, and I immediately regretted saying them.

The worst thing was that I never got to see Grandmother when I made it to sweet sixteen, the age she mentioned, because she died a couple years before that when she was sixty-two. I tried to make it up to both of them after what happened that day, and I'm glad I did. Mom accepted my apology, but she said something I'll always remember: "You can forgive, but you can't forget." I don't believe she was laying a guilt trip on me. She was telling me how she felt. She always told people exactly how she felt.

When Grandmother had my aunt Monica, her youngest child, she was about forty-five, and they didn't have blood pressure medicine in those days, so she had her first stroke when she had her baby. She died of a stroke when my aunt was newly married and in her 20s. She moved into my aunt's house, and my aunt took care of her. I still miss my grandmother, Carmella.

To me, the funeral ceremony for Grandmother was grotesque and upsetting, putting my sweet grandmother on display for the world to see and gawk at when she had no idea, they were doing it or how she looked. "She looks so good," people said as they walked by the coffin and shook the hands of the family members in the receiving line.

"No," I wanted to scream. "She looks dead. How can she look good? Why the hell would you say that?" Instead, I stood there in shock that people could be so thoughtless. "Take that and stick it up your sorry ass," is what I wanted to say, but I didn't say anything because Mom and Dad were standing right there, and they'd blast me out for being disrespectful.

It was almost as bad as the saying, "Sorry for your loss" the main phrase people use these days when they're too lazy to think of anything else. I didn't lose my phone or keys, dummy. I lost a person I love.

I even remembered the name of the dead person in the viewing room next door to Grandmother. It was Cosmos Giordano. His young son was screaming for him to come back to life after he saw his dead body done up in a pin-striped, blue suit and red tie like he was ready to go to a fancy restaurant and order lobster, steak, and a cocktail.

It must have been weird for this dead man's son to see him with all that make-up plastered on his face. He definitely wouldn't wear it when he was alive, coaching soccer or taking his wife and kids out for ice cream. It was heart-wrenching, and I know how his son felt, so I patted him on the back and said I understood because my grandmother had just died too. In fact, she was in the next room if he wanted to see her. He shook his head no.

Cosmo's son stopped crying for a few minutes but then started up again when his uncle gave the eulogy for his dad. I tried to comfort him the best I could, but it was no use, so I went back to my grandmother's reposing room (that's what they called it. Can you believe it?) where people were still saying how good she looked. Some of these people never called or visited her when she was sick. But I guess that's the way most people are. They're always up for a funeral and the luncheon afterward, but they never have time to visit you when you're alive.

When my grandparents on my father's side died and everyone else went to the viewing, I decided to stay home by myself and held my own service for Nan Nan and Pop Pop by thanking God for giving them to me all those years and for all the fun times we had together at the farm, even the times that Pop Pop freaked out and Aunt Minnie had to carry me back to the bar piggyback saying, "Pop Pop's mad."

I thought about my grandfather bouncing me on his knee and pretending he was taking me on a trip to Naples, Venice, and Rome as he sang: "*Mee de deep o, A mee de dop o, la dalina di Pop Pop o.*" His pet name for me was "la dolly," (the dolly or doll baby and dalina in the song he made up). I loved it when my grandfather made up songs for me.

Thinking happy thoughts about my grandparents was a heck of a lot better than seeing their dead bodies laid out at the Galzerano Funeral Home in northeast Philly. However, I did go to St. Dominick's Church to see the priest give the Rites of Committal for both of them.

Nan Nan, who also died in her nineties, told Pop Pop at the gravesite that she'd miss him and tried to throw herself into the coffin with him, but my dad, Aunt Minnie, and Aunt Mary held her back. Uncle Tony didn't know what to do, so he stood there looking at the coffin. "Catty School," he said, "that's my father, and he isn't coming back."

I knew that the bodies of my loved ones were just a shell for their souls, but what I saw instead was an empty shell of who they once were when they lived on earth. Years later I read *The American Way of Death by* Jessica Mitford, and I understood that the funeral industry is exactly that, a business.

Some funeral directors help mourners by consoling them and memorializing the dead person, but the whole scenario is too much for me. I'd rather remember how people I cared about looked when they were alive. It's depressing seeing people we love when they're dead. In my case, it traumatized me for a long time.

My reactions to dead people and funerals probably started when I saw Mr. Galecki, Dad's customer at the bar, pretending he was dead, and I never got over it. I guess Uncle Tony would call it one of my *relsteens* or strange habits; maybe a mental health professional would call it a form of OCD, but most of us have at least one weird habit, and that's ok, I guess, if it doesn't interfere with the rest of our lives.

After Dad's father and mother died and he was left without his parents and The Royal Gardens, he moped around the house for a few days and returned to his job at The Bucks County Lounge. He was always there when the owner called him to work extra hours. He asked many of his former customers to come see him there and gained a few new ones because of his outgoing personality and willingness to give them exactly what they wanted, including good advice on anything from raising deadbeat kids to marital problems that caused knock-down drag-out fights.

All those years of listening to Dr. Alex and the psychiatrists at the bar helped make Dad his customers' favorite, in addition to the empathy and caring ways that sprang from dealing with his own emotional issues over the years. Although Dad enjoyed getting out of the house to go to his new job, it was never the same as being the proprietor of The Royal Gardens. He loved being the proprietor, and it rankled him to be a lowly employee, what he called a *peon*, even though "Joe the Bartender" enjoyed the same fame at his new stomping grounds as he did at his old one.

Sometimes Mom and I went to visit Dad at work and sat at the awkward wooden table and chairs surrounding the bar. He'd bring us two colas and whip up tuna or egg salad sandwiches with a side of potato salad. He introduced us to some of the regulars, and they'd make a big fuss over us like we were celebrities because we were related to their beloved "Joe the Bartender." But it wasn't enough because he didn't have the same status or notoriety, he enjoyed for the years he worked at the bar. He didn't have the authority to set prices, approve menus, or throw people out if they deserved it, although they rarely did at his new place.

Dad worked for four years at The Bucks County Lounge. One day Aldo, the owner, told him out of the blue that his cousin Frankie needed a job and would take my father's place as a bartender and short-order cook. He said that Dad was a great employee and that he hated letting him go, but he was looking for somebody younger, and, after all, family comes first. I guess when you get old, some employers don't think you're as worthwhile as young people and you can't do the job. If you ask me, old people can do the job well too, if not better than young people.

Life was going smoothly at 505 Azalea Lane. Who would have guessed that major changes were coming? I've learned from my years living at The Royal Gardens that that's the way life is. You never know what's going to happen, so it's best to take it as it comes, the good and the bad. You're better off doing that than running all kinds of "What if's" through your brain.

Chapter Thirteen
Something Wasn't Right

"Better days are coming. It won't always be like this."
—Mom to Dad after he lost his job

Dad was devastated and so were the regulars at the bar. Dad had to leave his job in two weeks, and my parents barely had time to process it. On his last day he took off his apron, hung it on the hook at the bar, and Mom and I picked him up in his silver Chrysler. By then, we only had one car because Dad refused to spend money on a new one every year like he did before. His one luxury was that big fancy car. My parents couldn't afford to buy one anymore because they didn't have much money coming in, and Dad had no prospects for a new job in his sixties.

My father was getting old and starting to show his age. The creases in his skin were deeper and more prominent, and his glorious silver hair took on a pale, yellow cast that was reflected in his once-ruddy complexion. He argued less with Mom and didn't pick on my brother and me as much about the filthy tub and letting the dog run wild. I wondered if he was going into a full-blown depression like the one he said he suffered in college. On the other hand, he was the best dad to our sister Theresa. She never knew the dad we had known all our lives because by then he was growing into a different person, a more docile and passive one, and that disturbed us more.

Not having a steady job began to eat away at Dad. Every day he'd ask Mom if she thought he'd be able to find a new job at his age and what we'd do for money if he didn't. Maybe we'd be out in the cold, or, even worse, Mom would have to find a job as a cook, waitress, or even a bartender, God forbid. He fretted about how she'd handle all the characters at the bar and stewed about how guys would flirt with her, but I knew that she could deal with whatever came her way. She was always the strong one.

Mom gave Dad her usual spiel of "Better days are coming. It won't always be like this. Things change. The more you worry, the less chance you'll have to get a new job." He'd pretend to suck it up and gave her his Alfred E. Newman of Mad Magazine "What me Worry?" look and push his middle fake tooth out with his tongue so it looked like he had no tooth at all. But it was hard for him to mask his true feelings. He'd sit there, close his eyes, and shake his head. He even cried once, just like a little kid. It made me sad to see him because he never cried, even when his parents died. Nothing affected him like the idea of not having a job and not being able to support his family.

My parents had more expenses with the house, and he'd probably go stark raving mad if his identity as "Joe the Bartender" was wrenched away from him permanently. He lived, breathed, and thrived on working in a bar, schmoozing with the customers, and acting as a friend and advisor to "his people." This motley crew was his tribe, and he'd feel lost without them. It would have killed him to not have that to look forward to every day. His reason for living was in jeopardy.

That sent Mom into action mode. She told me she was secretly sending out feelers to help him find a new job. She asked a few friends from her bridge club, and about the luncheons she gave at the restaurant for the ladies' club members to keep their ears open for job leads. One of Dad's pals was the one to turn the tide. It turns out that Jake from Dad's after-hours bar-hopping days knew of a bar right in Langhorne looking for a part-time bartender with a following who knew how to make sandwiches. Dad went to Morty's Tavern for an interview and came out a happy man.

Morty, the owner, had heard of Dad, who was a legend in the area, and hired him on the spot. Morty's place was smaller than The Royal Gardens and The Bucks County Lounge, so from the beginning, Dad felt at home there and not overwhelmed as he sometimes did at the bigger bars. Their sandwich offerings were limited to grilled cheese, meatballs that came from a food distributor, deli turkey and cheese, and sides of prepared potato salad, so Dad could concentrate on mixing drinks and serving foamy draft beers in mugs. There were no fries, onion rings, or any labor-intensive sides to worry about, just the basics, and Dad was fine with that.

The only things Dad didn't like was that some of the patrons called him "Pops." He was getting older but didn't want to admit it despite the signs of aging that seemed to worsen daily. Now he had a slight stoop and walked with a shuffle. He looked different from when he used to race around the bar waiting on a few customers at once, pouring beers, making change, and giving customers his take on what was happening in their lives.

The guys at Morty's were mostly a younger crowd from local construction crews and businesses near the Neshaminy Mall in Bensalem, a few blocks away from The Royal Gardens. Patrons thought of my dad as a grandfather figure to confide in when they had problems they couldn't solve. As time went on, he began to advise his customers about their marital problems and issues their kids faced with school, like bad grades, getting in trouble in class, and bullying.

His customers talked and he listened. He was great at it and couldn't wait to wake up and go to work, where he held court every day with his admiring fans. Some of his patrons said he would have made an amazing psychologist. Morty trusted him completely with the business and left him in charge when he and his wife went to Florida for two weeks during the Christmas holidays. When Morty returned, he gave Dad a big bonus and told him he was the best employee he ever had.

Although Dad had a rough time after he was let go for a younger man from the Bucks County Lounge, he showed us how strong he was by not being defeated by it. He applied for another job and did his best at it until something beyond his control forced him to leave. Mom, my brother, and I noticed that besides the normal signs of aging, like slowing down and losing his appetite, something wasn't right. Dad wasn't the same.

As the days went by, Dad's naturally yellowish complexion turned into a jaundiced appearance. Even some people at the bar noticed it and told him to get to the doctor right away because it could mean liver problems, and Dad drank at least a case of beer every couple of days. When Mom insisted he see our family doctor and Joe and I seconded it, he said, "Doc will tell me to quit working and soak up some sun in Florida. That's not my idea of fun. I love to work and always have. It keeps me going. Doc might say I have a terminal disease and pump me with medicines that have wicked side effects. Forget doctors. Let me live the way I want to for as long as I have. Just bug off, all of you."

Chapter Fourteen
Ever After

"I've always loved you and always will,"
—me to Dad

In our family shortly after their birth, everyone is given their own song that a family member composes for that person alone. Often, one of us gets the inspiration to make up the song and it's so perfect for the person that no one questions it. Sometimes a couple of us get together and collaborate. Missy got a sad song with a lilting melody, maybe because she had colic as a baby and cried a lot.

The other kids got songs based on what we saw in them early on. If one looked Italian or had an Italian affect, she got an Italian-sounding song like my daughter Shayna's called "Tootsie (her nickname), How We Love You," sung to the melody of "Che La Luna," an old Sicilian song sung by Louie Prima and later by the old man in "The Godfather." The singer accompanied his version with suggestive hand gestures and made the whole wedding party laugh.

Daughter Lauren was always a lively soul, so she got a wild circus melody. These songs were part of our family history, and each kid enjoyed having their own song. Family members laughed at the original songs that followed them into adulthood, sometimes to their embarrassment. One of my nephews had a song that began: "You're a mean old monkey, you're a monkey face," and a jumpy, jazzy melody accompanied it.

Making up these songs and singing them helped give us a family history and brought us closer together. Mom and Dad made music and poetry an important part of our family heritage, and the songs we sang for each other and the poems we recited held special meanings for all of us.

I made up a song for my little sister Theresa called "There is No One in This World Like Theresa," and there truly wasn't. In time, Theresa took Mom's place as the family matriarch, hosting lavish dinners at her home in Reading, and later in her farmhouse in Oley, on all major holidays.

Time zipped by, and before we knew it, Theresa had grown into a smart, beautiful teenager. She had many boyfriends when she was in high school. One of them was a young man named Dean. My father loved to recite the Rudyard Kipling poem, "Gunga Din" to honor Dean, only he was making fun of him rather than praising him. He loved to recite his version of the poem and ended it by spitting out (literally), a line in the last stanza, "You Lazarushian leather, Gunga Din."

We never found out what that line meant, but Dad could have won an Oscar for his dramatic reading of the poem. He was a great orator, especially when he dug into one of Theresa' s boyfriends, whom he never considered good enough for her until her future husband John came along. My sister met John, the perfect match, in one of her classes when they attended Villanova University as science majors.

Within the next month, Dad became so weak he could hardly get out of bed, and against his loud protests, Mom drove him to the family doctor in his silver Chrysler. The doctor took one look at his complexion, saw how exhausted he was, and sent him immediately to Dr. Diamandis, a noted oncologist. The specialist took Mom and me into a room that had only two chairs and a desk. It looked like a prison interrogation room that you see on TV. The nurse took Dad into another room to check his weight, which was way down, and blood pressure, which was way up.

Dr. Diamandis told us he believed, pending a few tests, that Dad had liver cancer. As soon as the tests came in, he would let us know the prognosis. Mom asked if it was curable. Without hesitation, the physician said that in most cases it wasn't because once the liver was affected, it was difficult, if not impossible to cure.

The phone rang and Dr. Diamandis answered it. He raised his second finger to tell us to wait. "It's the lab," he said. "They have the results."

After talking to the lab people and assessing the results, the oncologist told us to sit down. I could tell something bad was coming. Mom clenched a tissue with one hand and held on to my arm with the other. The doctor lowered his eyes. "I'm sorry to tell you this, Mrs. Spinelli, but your husband has cholangiocarcinoma, cancer of the bile duct. I'm afraid it's terminal."

"How long does he have, doctor?" she asked.

"About six months, give or take some time," Dr. Diamadis said.

"Is there anything you can do to stop it?" I asked.

"We could give him bypass surgery, but that would only buy him a little time. I think you should call hospice, and they could help him live for as long as he has more comfortably."

"We'll go with the bypass," Mom said.

"We'll set it up," the doctor said, flipping through his calendar.

"Now for the hard part," the doctor added.

"What do you mean? Isn't this hard enough?" I asked in my grumpiest voice.

"Do you want me to tell him about his condition, or do you want to tell him yourself?" he asked Mom, ignoring me. "I could be here with you if you choose to tell him yourself," he said.

Mom didn't give me a chance to answer. "We're not telling him," She said with certainty. "He's not in a good mental state. He may harm himself."

"Mom," I shouted, "You have to tell him."

Mom shook her head. "He knows something's wrong already. Telling him he's terminal would make it worse, and he wouldn't be able to live with it."

I reached for her hand, but she pulled it away. "We aren't telling him."

I looked at the doctor and shrugged.

"A few, but not many people, choose not to tell the patient, but I believe that everyone deserves to know the truth," the doctor said. "Think about it and let me know what you want to do."

Mom looked into the doctor's eyes without blinking. "We're not telling him." When Mom made up her mind, that was it.

He gave her a card with the number to the local hospice and said he'd set up the arrangements.

"Mom," I said, giving it one last ditch effort, "he must know that hospice is where you go to die. How will you keep it from him?"

"I'll worry about that later. For now, we're not telling him. I want him to have the bypass surgery as soon as possible so we can give him more time."

"Remember, it won't give him much time," Doctor Diamandis said. "I'm here if you need me. Call me if you do. I'll take you to his examining room."

"Thank you, doctor," Mom said in a shaky voice. I didn't say anything because by this time I was ticked off because Mom didn't want him to know he was going to die soon. I followed her to the room where Dad waited for us, probably hoping a prescription or a shot would make him better.

The first thing he said when he saw us was, "I want to feel like my old self again. I'll do whatever it takes."

We never told Dad he was dying, but we heard later, after he died, that a man he knew at the barber shop somehow knew what was wrong with him (bad news travels fast) and leaked the

fact that Dad had a bad form of cancer to Dad. My father never said anything to us about the conversation in the barber shop, and that must have been painful to him. But he kept quiet and spared us the agony of letting us know what he found out. I wish that one of us had told him in a quiet, compassionate way that didn't include his discovering his terrible fate in a crowded barber shop.

Meanwhile, Theresa's wedding was weeks away. She and John had made plans for a lavish wedding and reception at Villanova's campus, but because of Dad's illness and poor prognosis, they had to change their plans drastically. Theresa and John ended up getting married at Our Lady of Grace, our local parish, with a favorite Villanova priest officiating. They had a simple reception at Georgine's, a local restaurant.

Theresa and all the attendants wore dresses that Mom made herself, bordered in ruffles and done up in delicate shades of pink. All the attendants, including my daughters, Melissa and Shayna, along with the groom's sister Dee, wore pink. As the matron of honor, I wore deep magenta. My youngest daughter Lauren wore a flower girl's gown of light pink and magenta, made from the remnants of the bridesmaids' gowns.

Since my father had become very weak by that time, my brother Joe walked our sister down the aisle. One thing that upset Dad during his illness was the thought that he wouldn't be able to walk Theresa down the aisle when she married her fiancé, John.

As it turned out, Dad was okay with my brother walking her down the aisle, and he was still able to stand in the reception line outside the church to greet all the guests who showed up in the receiving line. Despite his terminal illness, he was great at making people feel at ease by asking them about their families and what was happening in their lives. Most of them never guessed anything serious was wrong with him.

It was the best wedding, and I got to pick out the music for the guitarists. For the opening song, I chose "Morning Has Broken" by Cat Stevens. We danced the night away at Georgine's Restaurant; Dad sat at a table with us and rejoiced that his baby daughter had finally found a young man he liked.

Shortly after the ceremony, Dad made it through the bypass surgery, but the doctor called to tell us the disease had progressed to the point where he had only a short time to live. I could never accept that Mom wouldn't tell Dad he was going to die, and I resented her for it. During his final days, I felt that Dad knew he was going to die, especially after he heard the news in the barber shop, but he never let on to any of us.

He went on with his exercise routine, ate healthy foods, and acted more positively than I've ever seen him. When the hospice nurses came to our house, he acted like we'd hired them from a nurses' agency. They never said who they were (Mom's orders), and he never asked about it. He probably knew, after the man in the barber shop divulged his condition, but I think he guarded Mom's desire that he shouldn't ever know.

The only hint he gave that he might know he was dying is saying about a million times a day what he said to us that day in the hospital, "I want to feel like my old self again." He also said, "When I get flushed, I'm going to buy a big filet mignon and invite everyone in our family to dinner or take us on a trip to Italy where we could visit my parents' birthplace," but none of these things ever happened.

Dad suddenly started exercising rigorously every day, like a madman, forcing himself to jog in place, do jumping jacks, and touch his toes until he broke into a raging sweat. When he looked like he was about to collapse, he fell into his favorite lounge chair and said that's all he could take for one day, but he never gave up. He became more jaundiced each day as the illness progressed.

Then, one afternoon, Mom called to tell me that she thought Dad had

had a stroke when he was taking a nap because his mouth was sloping downward and he wasn't talking, just lying in bed and not moving. I felt paralyzed and couldn't move, so I called my daughter Melissa to go over to see what was going on. My mother did not wait to call the rescue squad, but by the time Melissa got there, Mom had called them, and the ambulance was loading Dad on to a gurney. To this day, I wish I'd answered Mom's call and spared Melissa the pain of seeing him like that and having to deal with it.

I met Mom and Melissa at St. Mary's hospital, where they told us it was only a matter of time until he died. When we were alone in the room, I held his hand, which was black and blue from the IV and told him that despite all our problems and the fights we had I always loved him and that I would forever after. I know he heard me because he looked right at me and smiled before he closed his eyes and never woke up.

I left St. Mary's with Aunt Minnie. Only Mom and Joe remained at his bedside. Aunt Minnie called us soon after to tell us that dad had died. She said he'd waited to die until we'd left to spare us the pain. I think she was right.

We had a service for Dad at the Bradley funeral home the night before the Mass. Luckily, it didn't freak me out like my other experiences viewing dead bodies did, because this time I only peeked and didn't linger at the coffin. Aunt Minnie and Aunt Mary stood by his coffin, and Mary said how good he looked. Dad would have told her to shut up because he couldn't stand how she made everything so dramatic. Aunt Minnie cried quietly and tried to comfort me by rubbing my back. Uncle Tony kept looking at him and saying, "That's my brother, Catty School. He was my best friend."

"I know, Uncle Tony," I said, and my heart broke for him, wondering if he grasped the reality of it.

I knew that it was just his body lying there and believed his soul had already gone to heaven. A Mass of Christian Burial at Our Lady of Grace Church followed where they sang all his favorite hymns and ended with "Holy God, We Praise Thy Name," a hymn he blasted out in his loud, tone-deaf voice at eleven o'clock Mass at Our Lady of Grace Church every Sunday. He would have loved it.

Dad loved The Knights of Columbus, a Catholic fraternal group, and a bunch of them showed up at his service in full regalia, including fancy hats with colorful feathers and sabers. They presented Mom with a Bible that she kept for the rest of her life.

After Dad died, I began to consider the ever after part of death instead of all the sadness that accompanied the rituals we embraced to make ourselves feel better when they only made us feel worse. I remembered the spirits in The Roosevelt Cemetery saying, "Don't be afraid for us. It's all good. Things are better where we are now and much easier, so don't be afraid of life, death and ever after. It's all good."

I know in my heart that something about all of it is eternal and that we live on and still care about the people we've left behind, that they love and miss us and hated to leave this world despite all the problems they faced. I don't have all the answers. I don't know if there's eternal life in paradise, reincarnation, or something we don't have the brain power to figure out, but I know that we live on in the spirit world and that they are always with us.

There's something that lives on in Dr. Alex, Mr. Galecki, my grandparents, and my dad, and I don't believe it because of what the spirits in Roosevelt Cemetery or my intuition told me, and I don't believe it because of all the times I memorized The Baltimore Catechism or what the priests said when they came to our house for dinner to eat Mom's crab cakes with a side of spaghetti and homemade orange cake for dessert. You know how you know something's true, and you don't need to question it? You know it in your gut and in your soul's core. Do you feel that way too? I wonder how many people do.

Chapter Fifteen
Better Days are Coming.

"Take a shower first thing in the morning and put on pretty clothes and make-up. It sets the tone for your whole day."
— Mom's advice to me

Mom lived alone in her house at Azalea Lane for twenty-four years after Dad died. During those years Mom kept busy getting her grandkids off to school, helping me keep the household running while I worked as a teacher, and hosting Sunday dinners. She loved spending time going to bridge club with her friends, shopping at the local mall for new clothes. She had a great fashion sense, and all her friends complimented her on outfits she put together.

After she'd lived alone for over two decades, Mom began to find it difficult keeping up with the demands of her ranch house at Azalea Lane. After she fell in the front yard and lay there for a long time waiting for help, she decided to move to an independent living facility called Green Valley, where she'd have nurses and doctors nearby if she ran into trouble. She already knew a few women from her bridge club who had moved there and looked forward to playing cards and eating dinner with them.

Dinner was always a big event where everyone dressed up and shared stories about their children and grandchildren. The ladies enjoyed going shopping at the local mall for new fashions for upcoming events at Green Valley, like the spring dance where the women outnumbered the men, cocktail hour, bridge tournaments, or a wine and cheese party. There was always something going on that kept the residents busy and made them forget, if only for a short time, about their aches and pains.

I visited Mom often in her cozy one-bedroom apartment at Green

Valley, and she'd cook me a spaghetti dinner, or I'd bring something from home like shrimp I'd cooked. She'd always say, "I wish I had more of that. It was delicious," and I wondered if she meant it or was trying to make me feel good, as she always did. It reminded me of the times she'd bake her fancy decorated Christmas cookies, and I'd make my easy lemon bars and she'd say, "I hope you're baking your famous lemon bars. I can't wait to eat them."

Mom was safe in her new home, and I was happy for her. No more working twelve-hour days at the Royal Gardens or caring for Dad during his last illness. She said she'd never marry again. Though she loved Dad despite all his problems, she wanted to have a few years where she could do what she wanted when she wanted, and that's exactly what she did. Mom always believed that better days were coming, even after all she went through.

Around this time, I'd retired from my job as a teacher/department head for the School District of Philadelphia and from my position as a student teaching supervisor at Temple. Our three daughters were grown, and two had their own careers and their own children, and I was a Nonna (grandmother of five). I never sat on the couch like my grandparents during retirement but forged a career as a writer of non-fiction books.

Everything seemed to be going smoothly just as it always does, when smack in the middle of it, something went wrong. One spring afternoon with the sun shining and all was well with the world, I went to the independent living place to see Mom and my sister Theresa to meet Dr. Emily Gladstone, the new geriatric doctor who would help us find some solutions for her health problems, which included COPD and high blood pressure.

Dr. Gladstone would replace the one she had that was getting harder for her to visit. He was far away from Green Valley, and she had to depend on someone to drive her, which she hated. She also thought that having her own geriatric doctor at Green Valley might offer better insights into her growing health problems. After we met the new doctor, my sister planned to drive Mom to Boscov's, her favorite department store, to buy summer clothes, and then they'd go out for lunch.

That's not the way it played out. When the facility's staff brought Mom down on the elevator to the health suite, they forgot to bring her oxygen tank. They immediately put her on the scale and tried to weigh her. Isn't that the first thing they always do when you go to a doctor's office?

Meanwhile, my sister and I were in the doctor's office talking to my mom's new doctor, about how happy we were that mom would have a geriatric doctor who would help her with her age-related medical issues. Suddenly, we heard a blood-curdling scream. I wondered who could be screaming like that and why. An aide hurried in and told us that while getting on the scale, Mom had fallen and landed on the hard, linoleum floor. Who would have thought?

Dr. Gladstone, my sister, and I stopped talking and ran out to the hallway to see what was going on. We saw Mom writhing in pain and screaming, surrounded by staff members. We were shocked that it was Mom because she was perfectly ok when the nurses brought her down to the medical suite on the elevator. A nurse said that an ambulance would arrive in a matter of seconds to rush her to St. Mary's Hospital. After the ambulance came and sped Mom to the hospital, Dr. Gladstone, who was going to take over her care, told us that when Mom got out of the hospital, they'd move her temporarily to the nursing home within the Green Valley complex because she wouldn't be able to do anything for herself. It wouldn't help to put her in assisted living since she'd need specialized care to help her heal from severe injuries due to the fall.

My sister hurriedly packed a few of Mom's clothes, and we rushed to St. Mary's Hospital where we found Mom in excruciating pain, waiting to be examined by an orthopedic surgeon. After the doctor examined her, he said she'd broken her femur in the fall from the scale and would need three surgeries. I could tell she was fearful about going under anesthesia to have the surgery, and we did our best to reassure her.

We stayed until she got a room and promised to return tomorrow before the operation. On the way out, my sister Theresa asked me how I could remain so calm after Mom fell. I told her that I was in shock and couldn't believe this happened to Mom. All along, I wondered why the nurses there forgot to bring her oxygen and made her stand on the scale for a weight check when she was so weak.

My sister arrived at the hospital before the first surgery and waited until it was over. It was a success, and the doctors told us that the second surgery was scheduled in a few days. Mom also came through that one beautifully. One more surgery remained. We brought Mom books, and she watched her favorite news programs and soap operas. Watching "Days of Our Lives" to see what was going on with Marlena and the rest of the gang took away some of the apprehension she had about the final surgery. Three is usually a charm, but I was apprehensive about the third surgery. My psychic sense warned me to be wary.

To make matters worse, Mom told us she saw my father, who had passed over twenty years ago, sprawled out in the chair next to her hospital bed—definitely not a good sign. When someone sees a deceased loved one, it often means that person is coming to take them with them to the spirit world.

I wasn't ready to say good-by to Mom yet. She was eighty-five, but she was getting her health problems under control, and she was enjoying life as she hadn't been able to in many years because of Dad's mental and physical problems. Now she lived among friends, and we visited her often. She loved shopping, searching for spiffy outfits at Boscov's, and going out to lunch; and she looked forward to spending time with her family and friends. Mom couldn't leave us, not yet, until she had a few more years of happiness without having to worry about anything. Her life was starting to improve before her fall, and we wanted it to continue.

My sister and I left the hospital that night apprehensive about the outcome of that third surgery. Were our fears justified, or would she come through it? I slept fitfully that night, awaiting the call from my sister, who would tell me that everything had turned out well and that Mom would be transferred to the nursing home at Green Valley in a couple of weeks. The next morning Theresa called me. She was crying, and all she said was "Cath," one of Mom's nicknames for me. I knew then that Mom hadn't come through the surgery.

"Those bastards," I said, referring to the aides at the independent living place who didn't bother to bring her oxygen to the medical suite and propped her up on the scale before she suffered a catastrophic fall. The doctor said she'd died of a pulmonary embolism when they tried to repair her broken femur. The rest of the family went to the hospital to see Mom one last time, but I didn't go. I couldn't bring myself to see her after she'd died. What was the use, anyway? She was gone. I called her surgeon afterwards to ask how this could happen.

He was a young, empathetic doctor who told me that he hated to perform this surgery on older patients as there was a chance they could die from a heart attack or a blood clot, as Mom did. He told me that he'd asked a cardiologist, who was operating on someone in the next surgical suite, to see if there was anything he could do to help her, but it was all in vain.

Somehow, I got through making plans for Mom's funeral. Lauren, our youngest daughter, sang Mom's Mass in her heavenly voice. Everyone cried when she sang "How Great Thou Art," the closing hymn. Mom had a closed coffin as she requested. I made sure I got there after they opened it briefly for the family. Like all the other family members who left the earth before me, I wanted to remember her as she was: living: breathing, talking, and laughing, not as a lifeless body.

After the Mass, we went to Piccola Trattoria, a cheery bistro in a strip mall near my house where I read the eulogy I'd written for Mom. Here's the text:

"Where did you come from?" Mom once asked me. She often repeated a story about some wild, exotic creature named Chiquita Maguita, who surely must have spawned me,
someone so different from Mom. Catherine Louise, or Cath, as she called me, could never have sprung from her.

Mom and I were polar opposites. She loved embellishing her home with freshly cut flowers from her garden. I hated weeding and squiggly worms. She loved the peacefulness of staying home rather than fighting the 9-5 rat race, and I loved the excitement of going to my job. She transformed her home into a spread from "House Beautiful" while I still struggle to swim out of the clutter.

Mom was a proper lady who wore dresses until her friends convinced her to ditch them for pantsuits. "I'm mortified that you'd go out to the store in those tight biker pants you wear to exercise," she'd say, shaking her head.

"If you've got it, flaunt it," I'd shoot back, and she'd crack up.

She always accepted her religion and had unconditional faith, while I questioned and probed and wondered still what it's all about, who we are, and where we're heading. She called my love of the psychic world "Hocus Pocus" and thought it was spooky that I read Tarot cards.

One thing she loved was Reiki healing, but she loved it even better when I'd rub her back with a feather touch, reaching all the right places.

We were different, Mom and I, but we also had a lot in common. She loved her kids and grandkids unconditionally, more than life itself, and has passed that down to me. We enjoyed many discussions about books, current events, and the meaning of life.

She and I both shared a love of cooking comfort food, like lasagna and devilled crab. I will miss calling her and asking her cooking questions, which I did until the day before she died when she told me my grandmother Nan Nan's roasted potatoes tasted delicious because she cooked them in lard.

I try to follow her advice about looking decent before leaving the house. "You never know who you might run into," she'd say. "Take a shower first thing in the morning, put on pretty clothes and make-up. It sets the tone for your whole day." And she was right.

The most important lesson Mom taught me is that no matter how hard life becomes, you need to keep moving forward and never give up. "Stagger onward rejoicing" as the poet Auden said. Ultimately, things will get better if you are willing to stick it out. "Better days are coming" was always her mantra.

We were both always acutely aware of our own mortality, of the tenuousness of life. That is why our family was always so important to both of us, why I believe it's important to cherish each moment with the family and friends we love; why we shouldn't wait until they die to really look at them, to tell them we love them and how we cherish that love, no matter how corny that sounds to some people.

As Emily, the lead character, asked in "Our Town," a play Mom loved: "Do any human beings ever realize life while they live it—every, every minute?" That's what Mom gave to all of us, the urgency of living every moment, of being totally *in* the moment. That's how she acted when we were there with her, as if nobody and nothing else mattered. She was always present for us, and I believe that wherever she is, she always will be. "

During our years living at the bar, she taught me that even though she was stuck in a job she didn't love, she was able to see the positive side of it and always made the best of every situation she faced, mainly dealing with Dad's issues and her relationship with him. She loved him until the end, and I think he felt the same despite having to deal with his emotional issues.

Living at the bar and talking to the spirits in the Roosevelt Cemetery taught me the benefits of using my intuitive muscles and eventually led me to do psychic work in a local tearoom and my friend's boutique, "Blue Sky in the Morning." I eventually taught full time in high school in a city school district and part-time at Temple University, mentoring student teachers. I kept my psychic powers in the background so as not to alienate the establishment. However, psychic skills came in handy whenever I needed additional insights into the problems I faced daily on the job.

Mom always said that better days were coming. Her life and death told me that if we wait long enough they actually will.

Chapter Sixteen
All Couples Fight: Reprise

"Now your troubles will begin, Caterina."
—my father-in-law Peter to me while we danced as my wedding

A couple of years after Theresa entered our world, I met my future husband, Andrew. We met in a snowstorm at the W.T. Grant shopping center in Levittown, PA, when I was 18 and a college freshman at Temple University, and he was 24 and working as a social worker. It sounded a lot like how my parents met when they were more than a few years apart. That night we were stranded in a snowstorm at the Levittown mall, and I abandoned my car in the parking lot. A co-worker gave me a ride home on the icy roads.

Andrew and Jim, his fraternity buddy from college, had come to visit their friend, Carl, who worked there as an assistant manager. Andrew was tall, lean, and handsome with dark hair, dreamy hazel eyes, and a warm smile. He spotted me from the staircase that led to the housewares department where I made keys and sold pots and pans and wine glasses.

Our eyes met for a brief moment, and I thought, "Someday I'm going to marry that guy," even though we hadn't met yet. Love at first sight, you could say, like Joe, the Bartender and Mary Grace and Aunt Mary and Josh. I remember what I was wearing that day, a straight checkered blue/gray skirt and a royal blue crew neck sweater. He wore a pair of khaki slacks and a two-toned light and dark gray sweater.

Even though I lived in a bar in my early years, I still couldn't identify a wine glass and knew nothing about houseware or making keys, which were among my duties working in the hardware department at WT Grants. I worked with a hefty woman named Mabel, who had to hang from a contraption for her sore neck (she called it *traction*) for a few hours a day. I was in charge of houseware every time Mabel decided she needed her treatment, which was a major part of the workday.

I had to fend for myself, discussing with customers, among other things, how to choose the best wine glasses. You'd think I would have known about wine glasses after living in a bar, but those things didn't matter to me back then. I was far more interested in talking to and psychoanalyzing the characters who came in the bar each day, just as they loved trying to figure out who this quirky, sassy child was who loved to watch Howdy Doody on our postage stamp-sized TV. I'd advise the bar patrons on everything from the state of the world to the stuff I learned from Miss Clara about God and the afterlife and what I thought of it all. "You've got yourself a handful," they'd tell my parents. "She's old beyond her years."

"We wouldn't have it any other way," Dad said.

Andrew, the mystery mam looking at me from the top of the stairs, came to my rescue when I didn't know how to identify a wine glass. He rushed down the stairs as he saw me struggle when I tried to answer a customer's question. He held one up and said, "Here's what you're looking for, right?" to the disgruntled customer. She smiled and said "Yes, now why couldn't *she* have told me that?" eying me as if I were a total incompetent.

"Mabel's in traction and I'm just learning," I said. She asked me what the heck I was talking about, and I handed her the glasses wrapped up in newspapers and a Grant's plastic bag, just as Mabel had taught me. She left shaking her head, but not before thanking the handsome young man who gave her what she came into W.T. Grant's for.

Andrew and I started talking and we hit it off instantly. He had just graduated from college as a business major and was waiting for a job in marketing, his major field. He currently worked as a social worker for the state of New Jersey because he couldn't find a job in business. I was a freshman at Temple, majoring in English education, hoping to get a position as a high school teacher.

Aunt Mary's experience teaching lurked in the back of my mind and made me wonder if I had the guts to do it. I kept telling myself that I was not Aunt Mary and could deal with any problems that would come my way. At least, that's what Mom taught me. "There's always a way to get what you want," she'd say. "Don't let anything stop you from landing your dream job. You have the knowledge, drive, and ambition, and can get any job you desire."

I signed out of work, and while I waited for my co-worker to drive me home, Andrew and I talked for a long time near the WT Grant's entrance. He took my number and agreed to call me soon. As it turned out, he lost my number, but he remembered that it was similar to one of his ex-girlfriend's phone numbers and finally called in a week. When I got home that night after a treacherous ride in the ice, slipping and sliding in my snowy driveway, my boyfriend Matt was sitting on our living room couch waiting for me. Mom hugged me and said how happy she
was that I got home safely. Then she left Matt and me alone to talk about the possible ending of our two-year relationship.

He'd stopped by Grant's earlier that night to discuss our break-up shortly before. I told him that I wanted to end our relationship, but he wouldn't take *no*, and later he met me at 505 Azalea Lane. Since he was going to college far away in Florida, I told him that a long-distance relationship wouldn't work, but he thought we should try it. I wasn't willing, so we broke it off. It was hard because we were high school sweethearts, but I thought a break-up now would save more tears later. It took a long time to convince him, and I don't think he ever believed it. He's been happily married to a classmate for years, so I guess he was wrong.

When Andrew finally remembered my phone number, we made a date to see a movie called "Taurus Bulba with Tony Curtis and Yul Brenner." It was about a Cossack chief and his misadventures, and I found it boring beyond belief. We'd decided to go on a double date with his friend Carl and his girlfriend. I found Andrew charming and gallant, but the moment we got inside the movie theater, I wish I'd never consented to go out with him after what happened next.

The movie dragged on, and I couldn't stay awake, no matter how much popcorn I ate or cola I drank. When Andrew reached for my hand, I jumped up startled. I think I shocked him because he looked like he was thoroughly enjoying the movie. By the time the movie was over, he helped me into the car, but we didn't talk much on the way home.

Andrew's friend Carl said later that he could feel the tension between us (I think he saw me dozing off in the movie. I hope I didn't snore.) I wondered if this was a harbinger of things to come. Should we see each other again? I'll bet Andrew wondered too.

Later Andrew told me that he felt embarrassed because I fell asleep in front of his friends. I said that I was tired from working in the hardware department all weekend and that it had nothing to do with the movie. Big lie!

Our next date, a cozy steak and seafood dinner in a secluded county inn, called The Ewing Riding Club, went a lot better. Andrew drank white wine, and I had a cherry coke because I couldn't tolerate alcohol, probably from being raised in a bar.

Mimicking Dad and Mom's lightning-fire courtship, Andrew and I met during that snowy Christmas holiday in 1962, the year I graduated from high school, and we got engaged on Valentine's Day two months later. We planned a wedding for August 31 of that year. Most people these days don't have that quick a courtship, but we found ourselves deeply in love and decided to get married.

My dad and Andrew became fast friends. Dad loved his strong work ethic. He was working on his master's and ultimately decided to teach business in Philly after a brief stint teaching social studies in the suburbs. Born in New Haven, Connecticut, he was a city person at heart. He loved teaching with a passion and ultimately taught day school, night school, and summer school. Mom loved Andrew too and made him foods he enjoyed, like sausage and peppers and her famous lasagna (see recipe at the back of this book).

If we wanted a church wedding we had to meet with Father Bonner, the parish priest at Our Lady of Grace, who would advise us on how to conduct our lives according to the Catholic rules of Matrimony. (We found out he later married a parishioner and abruptly left the priesthood.) I wondered if our marriage was then null and void.

He told us during our pre-Cana conferences that he expected us to follow all the rules of the church dealing with contraception and that it would be a good idea to quit any job I had when I began to have babies, as a woman's main purpose in life was to serve her husband and to provide a happy home for the oodles of kids we'd bear. He also said that after I had about three children, I should come see him to review approved methods of birth control so I wouldn't live in mortal sin and be damned to hell forever, God forbid.

We yessed Father to death but ended up doing our own thing because we weren't so clueless that we'd listen to a man who'd never married or had kids for family planning advice. We got married at Our Lady of Grace Church with Andy's cousin Virginia, my best friend Carol, and his friends Carl and Jim, who were with us the night we met, in attendance. His younger brother, Anthony, served as best man. We gave a small reception at the Golden Horse Inn, which was right next to the Royal Gardens on Roosevelt Boulevard. Miss Laura and a few of Dad's friends at the bar attended.

As a new bride, I danced with Andrew, and then my new father-in-law, Peter, the quietest person I've ever met. We were slow dancing when Peter looked into my eyes and said six words: "Now your troubles will begin, Caterina." Why did he say these ominous words to me? Did he know something I didn't? I didn't know what he meant at the time, but those words haunted me for years. Was that what he thought of marriage? I'd heard he married his wife because his parents thought she was a good worker and knew how to handle money. Did they have a

romantic attachment, or was it a marriage of convenience? Later, I discovered it was a little of both, as many marriages were in those days.

We honeymooned in Atlantic City for a weekend and shared a dinner of spaghetti and meatballs and garlic bread at the Bella Napoli restaurant because we were short on funds due to the fact that Andrew was in grad school and working in his first job as a social worker. I was still a college freshman and had three years left before getting my degree. We moved down the road from Azalea Lane to the Penndel Court Apartments. I soon discovered that a strange conglomeration of people lived there. Of course, we had names for them, just as my parents had names for people at the Royal Gardens.

Among the cast of characters at Penndel Courts were "Southern Bell," a gracious lady married to a funeral director's apprentice who bragged about once slapping a corpse on the butt when his job stressed him out. Thank God, he soon got a job as a meat cutter at Shop and Bag. His fellow morticians would have driven him out for disgracing the profession.

Then there was "Big Boy," a gargantuan teenager who lurked outside our apartment and sang songs like "Puff, the Magic Dragon" and other folk songs he created himself.

Mom was visiting me one day and knew about Big Boy. She told him to get lost and to never come back or she'd call the police. We never saw him again, thank God. He must have gone back to school, or wherever he was supposed to be. That made the neighbors happy too.

Andrew and I had a lot of skirmishes during our first year in the apartment, probably due to the fact that I was in college and learning how to juggle my studies as a commuter to Temple with my tasks as a new bride. Although Andrew helped a lot around the house by cleaning up after dinner and doing laundry, I felt overwhelmed juggling my school duties and household chores.

During this period of adjustment, the residents threw a pool party and didn't invite us. I overheard one of them say through my open window, "They're a nice couple but all they do is fight." I didn't realize that's how they saw us, as two people who couldn't get along. I knew we were young and foolish, but I found their comments embarrassing and sad.

A couple times when our arguments got too loud, Southern Belle and her husband, we gave him the name Moo Moo Looba, for no reason at all, (other than it sounded goofy, and I thought he was a goofball), banged on our ceiling with a broom handle, hoping we'd tone it down a decibel. We never said anything about the banging broom handle afterward and neither did they, but we knew they were sending us a message. Besides, I was leery about Southern Belle's husband, Moo Moo Looba. If he smacked a corpse on their butts, what tortures would he dream up for us?

Chapter Seventeen
Good Times and Bad

"I can't take you two anymore."

—marriage counselor to us

After a few months, I found that I was expecting a baby. The pregnancy came earlier than we'd anticipated, but we were happy and excited. We planned on naming the baby boy Martin. Unfortunately, after a couple of months, I miscarried. We were deeply saddened by this terrible event. Soon after that, we had a flood in the apartment and had massive water damage. Mom kept telling us that "better days are coming," but I began to doubt it and wondered if and when they would appear.

"Hang in there," she'd say, and she believed it. I guess we had to wait and see, but Mom was usually right about everything.

The disruptions to our lives finally started easing up and we were able to feel comfortable with each other and not argue as much. However, we knew we needed help. We'd lived in Penndel Courts for three years, and we decided we were going to work on our communication skills, so we consulted Catholic Social Services and made an appointment with a social worker named Jay.

He was young like us, but we could tell from the beginning that he was inexperienced because he quickly lost patience with us, a couple who couldn't seem to agree on anything. After six visits, when he'd had enough, he said, "I can't take you two anymore. I know you may consider me unprofessional, but I have to give you my honest opinion. I hope you can find someone to help you. Maybe you should separate for a while and see how that goes. I don't think it's healthy for you to stay together, but don't quote me on it. You can't agree on much of anything."

Years later, in the 70s, I thought about how Al Green's song, "Let's Stay Together" that said "Good times and bad, happy and sad" fit our situation back then. When we were going through the turmoil, I hoped things would work out so we could stay together. I wondered how we would end up with all the crazy things that happened and how we reacted to one another when we faced solving problems.

Were there enough good times to hold us together, or would we end up in divorce court? I also thought about how when I was younger, I applied the word *unhealthy* to Mom and Dad's relationship. How important was it to have a healthy relationship, and would we pass the test?

I thought of Mom and Dad's marriage in relation to ours. Were their inharmonious interactions somehow rubbing off on us? Was history repeating itself? I certainly hope not, but we found it hard to agree on a lot of things. Jay was right about that.

Here are some of the ways we clicked. We liked to see shows, movies, eat good food, and dance together. We also enjoyed talking about psychology and current events. Most of all, despite being first-born children who were used to having their own way, we enjoyed one another's company, and we never fought about money, like Dad and Mom and many of our friends did.

Here are ways we differed, but it didn't stop us from staying together: Taking cues from Mom, I spend my life in the present and live for today. Yesterday is gone, and we're not sure if we have tomorrow. Andrew lives one step ahead, in the future. Andrew is quick in doing things and does everything at record speed. One of the students who accompanied us on a trip to Italy dubbed him "Speedy Gonzales," and I still call him that today. I like to take my time and do things carefully and deliberately, like Mr. Rogers, the TV neighborhood man of yore, while Andrew likes to get things done in a hurry. Strangely, we usually get the same results.

I guess there's much to say about both philosophies. In the end, it doesn't matter, as long as you get things done. Another difference is that Andrew is strong in his faith and rarely questions. I love to question everything, trying to discover why people think as they do and why institutions such as schools, churches, and government proclaim the theories they do. If I don't agree, I'll say so.

During our first year of marriage, the second counselor we saw, Dr. Tim McKenny, thought he was an expert and didn't mind flaunting it. When we left after the first session, he asked with a smug smile, "How did I do?" We left his office quickly, without answering his question, and never returned.

After the two negative experiences we had with marriage counselors, we decided to find our own ways of dealing with our issues. Although it didn't always resolve our problems, we dealt with them the best we could. Dear Abby's question about whether to stay in a relationship was always in the back of our minds: "Would I be better off with them or without them?"

We have three daughters and enjoy mutual love and respect for one another. Melissa, our oldest, has a great business sense and loves to write. Shayna, our middle daughter, works as a counselor, and Lauren, the youngest, writes for national publications, such as *The New York Times* and plans to publish a book.

For three generations, the women in our family gave birth to their last child with many years intervening between the child before. Grandmother Carmella, Mom's mom, had my aunt Monica at 45, when her other kids were grown; Mom had my sister Theresa in her late thirties; and I delivered Lauren, fourteen years after Melissa came into the world. I began to wonder if it was becoming a pattern. Regardless, it worked out well for all of us. The older sisters acted as second mothers to the later-born ones.

After we had our kids, juggling family life and jobs put new stresses and strains on our relationship. I started a job teaching English in a suburban school and hated it from day one. They grouped kids of all ability levels into one class (heterogeneous grouping). Attempting to appeal to a variety of ability levels, without boring advanced students or frustrating those who couldn't grasp the concepts fast enough, presented major challenges.

Naturally, that created a lot of behavior problems (echoes of Aunt Mary), and nothing I did worked to bring some of my classes to order. I didn't shout "Emergency, Emergency!" into the PA system as Aunt Mary did, but I gained a new appreciation for her sense of frustration working at Seaview High School and later in the suburban school from which I graduated. I flicked lights off and on, called parents, assigned detentions, and offered rewards, but nothing stopped the kids from calling out, falling asleep, and acting out. Teaching many different types of classes, (English 3, English 4, Spanish 1, Spanish 2, and Drama) didn't make it any easier.

I got no help from the administration, and the other staff members didn't reach out to help me find solutions. I was totally on my own in a new job for which two student teaching experiences (one in the suburbs, and one in the city) didn't prepare me. Maybe I wasn't cut out to be a teacher?

Had I wasted four years in college as an education major? Most of my teacher friends had trouble in their first year of teaching but not to the extent that I did. I went home every night feeling total frustration and went into work feeling the same way the next morning. Mom said, "Stick with it," and I tried my best. However, the writing was on the wall. I knew that I had to change jobs.

I applied for a job in the Philadelphia Schools, where the school system was more to my liking because it was diverse, and they didn't observe you every day without offering concrete suggestions on how to handle problems. They also let you use your creativity in implementing the curriculum.

Delivering instruction according to curricular guidelines was not static and lockstep. For instance, instead of giving pen and paper or multiple choice-tests, we were free to give alternative assessments in which each child working in the group would be evaluated on their individual contribution to the lesson.

We also had debates on current issues that honed students' research, writing, and public speaking skills. Teaching this way helped students become lifelong learners and also solved potential cheating problems because alternative assessments were cheat-proof. Teachers didn't have that freedom to choose how to deliver instruction when teaching in suburban schools during the 60s and 70s. City schools allowed teachers to be more creative.

After passing a written and oral test, which was more rigorous than the application process in the suburbs, administrators assigned me to Lincoln Junior High School. I later took the test for Lincoln Senior High School; I found teaching high school more rewarding than teaching middle school because I could have interesting conversations with the kids and there weren't as many discipline problems.

Meanwhile, after working in a suburban school district, the one where

I attended high school, Andrew found his first real teaching job and ended up teaching social studies. Luckily, a kind colleague and veteran teacher gave him tips that helped him survive working with a difficult middle school population, unlike his predecessor, who suffered nervous problems that led him to leave the job. Andrew wanted to teach business, his major, so he decided to seek a job in Philly, where he heard jobs had opened up. He landed a job teaching business in a city high school, and he found his niche.

I found teaching in a city school more rewarding than teaching in the suburbs. The administration and my co-workers were always available and supportive when problems came up; they made time to talk to me and offer suggestions that worked for them. For the most part, the students were appreciative and cooperative.

I disliked the fact that administrators often lumped all the troublemakers and rabble rousers in one class, but at least you knew what type of students you were getting by looking at the class number on the lists they handed you when they gave out your roster. The policy stayed the same for years and helped teachers know in advance if they were getting the class from heaven or hell by looking at the class number. On the other hand, I found the heterogeneous grouping that they had in the suburban school where I taught a difficult challenge. You never knew what kind of problem, academic or behavioral, you'd have to deal with. That made classroom instruction and management a major problem, especially for a new and inexperienced teacher.

As the years went by, Andrew and I continued to work at the same school on the outskirts of the city. We met a lot of interesting kids and parents. Many days when I was teaching literature, I thought of my father and wondered how he'd read and interpret a story or a poem (like Gunga Din) to help the kids love and remember it and make it part of their lives ever after. He and Mom gave me a love of literature that will stay with me always.

My parents also taught me how to truly listen to the students when they had a problem and needed advice as they did to everyone who came to visit the Royal Gardens. "Everyone has their own issues they're dealing with," Dad said, "so don't be quick to judge or tell them how you'd deal with their problem. Listen without lecturing and help them come to their own conclusion."

Mom was also the best listener who used eye contact and positive body language, so I took my cues from her when dealing with students, and it always worked out great. She'd listen to people who confided in her as if they were the only people in the room.

Something funny happened when we worked at our first school and Andrew taught night school. Uncle Tony appeared on the scene, smack dab in Andrew's face when he was teaching night school and strolling the hallway after work to leave the building. The head custodian had mentioned a few days earlier that Tony said he was related to two teachers who worked in the school district. He said that one was called "Catty School" and that she was married to Andrew. The head custodian made the connection although he'd never heard of anyone with the name "Catty School." He thought that was a rather strange name, but then, Tony was a funny kind of guy.

"Is this guy related to you?" the head custodian asked my husband. What the heck! Who could picture Uncle Tony having a job outside of working at the farm or the cabins?

Uncle Tony's boss said that he was a great worker and got along well with everyone and made people laugh. My uncle was pushing a broom in the hallway with lightning speed when he stopped to shake Andrew's hand. Unbeknownst to us, he was working as a custodian in different schools in the district for a couple of months after my grandfather sold the bar.

Uncle Tony wanted to find something to occupy his mind, since he wasn't in charge of the cabins anymore. Tony couldn't stand the routine of reporting for work every day. He missed his cubby in the basement that was stocked with Fig Newtons and chocolate milk. He also missed his lessons, which I was too busy to conduct since starting work.

Uncle Tony quit his job one spring day when the birds were singing and the sun shined down on the world, and he didn't look back. The head custodian tried to get him to stay because he was a conscientious worker, his best, but Tony said he had to move on because he had a better job waiting for him, which was eating Fig Newtons and drinking chocolate milk in his cubby, but his boss would never have guessed it wasn't true.

After a few years, Andrew and I both decided to take the tests for department head of our respective subjects, where you deal mainly with teachers, curriculum, and discipline and still teach a couple of classes. We loved being in the classroom, but we were ready for new challenges and responsibilities. To become a department head, you had to pass a written then an oral test, which was administered by principals and those who had worked for many years as department heads in city schools.

I studied for the written test and my psychic sense told me what I should concentrate on, and it helped give me an idea of the questions. I found out I'd passed the test when the union head called me and said, "Congratulations! You're the new English/world language department head at Rosa Parks High School."

She acted like I'd just scratched off a winning lottery ticket when, in reality, I'd been appointed department head at one of the most dangerous schools in the city. Rosa Parks High School was located deep in the heart of the inner city. The first day I drove there, I parked in the lot of a famous synagogue, where we were told our cars would be safe. When I came out to my old Honda to take the long trip home, I saw that a number of cars' windows were pick-axed. I ran to my car, expecting the worst. However, I was happy to see it wasn't damaged and nothing was amiss. Everything was just as I'd left it.

A young police officer inspecting the damages on the other cars said, "What a mess," he said. "It looks like you were spared the damages that all the other cars got. How did you do it?" he said, surveying the other cars and then looking at mine.

"The only thing I did was take the advice of a friend who once taught here. I left my car dirty and filled with junk so no one would be tempted to break the glass and look inside."

"Smart lady," said the officer. "Sounds like something I would do. I give you credit for working here. It's a war zone, Miss."

I smiled at him and took off for my hour ride back home. Was he telling me something I already knew, or was it a new warning to proceed with caution?

I enjoyed being a department head at Rosa Parks High School, although it was often challenging and nerve-wracking because many students either acted out in class or sat there, staring at the clock, waiting for the bell to ring so they could go to their jobs, tend their own children, or hang out with their friends. Once before class started, I found a student there I'd never seen before. I asked for his ID, and he said, "I just got back from incarceration." I calmly told him that he needed an ID to enter my class, and he left quickly.

Grandparents and social workers in group homes often acted as parents to our students, and if you tried to call homes to discuss a student's academic or behavioral issues, it was hard to reach anyone, or if you did finally get in touch with them, to gain insight into their problems. Often, grandparents caring for the kids were overwhelmed, and case workers had unmanageable caseloads, so it was hard for them to get back to you.

What did Mom say about my job's challenges? It was always this or a variation of it: do the best you can with the resources you have, and whatever you do, don't get too riled up because it doesn't help. If Dad were still alive, he would probably have gotten upset and started cursing. He may have said the "F" word. At least it would have made him feel better, or would it? He'd probably say, "Get the hell out of there as soon as you can. No job is worth that kind of aggravation."

Andrew was assigned a different inner-city school, down the road from Rosa Parks, my school, for his department head's job in the business department. He also found his hectic routine challenging. We'd both come home exhausted, and then he'd rest for a few minutes, exercise, eat on the run, and make the long trip back to the city for his night school stint.

As it turned out, I was at Rosa Parks High School for less than three years. The principal decided to drop all the department heads and appoint charter coordinators to save money. Coordinators wouldn't have the expertise to oversee curriculum or observe teachers and evaluate their performance as department heads did. To the principal, money was the bottom line. Was it that important to have quality control over the curriculum, and how could you tell if teachers were doing their job, was his way of thinking.

He kept an obsequious young math teacher as department head who kowtowed to him as the lone department head in the school. The rest of us were shipped out to other schools. I was in the system for over twenty-five years and went to the Board of Education to choose a new department head's position in another school. There was an opening at Girls' High School, an academic high school, which was one of two girls' public high schools in the country, so I applied there, hoping I'd get assigned to the school that everyone in the city wanted to work in.

The Philadelphia High School for Girls is an academic magnet school, and one of the first public high schools for women. The school's motto, "*vincit qui se vincit*," means *she conquers who conquers herself.* From the day I entered this school, I knew that the motto embodied everything it represented. The students were outgoing, cheerful, and worked to their fullest capacities to achieve academic excellence. Students and faculty alike did everything to make me feel at home when I was assigned the job. Unlike my other schools, there were no discipline problems, cheating episodes, or fights in the hallways. I was in teaching heaven.

Andrew and I took a group of students from Girls' High to Italy, and our daughter Lauren came along. We had a rollicking time seeing all the sights, including visiting the Vatican, riding a gondola through the canals of Venice, and viewing St. Francis' church in Assisi, where the saint's remains rest.

We also drove through Amalfi, Grandpa Peter's birthplace, which Andrew loved. However, the downside of the trip was our hotel. Lauren, our daughter, stayed in the hotel in Sorrento with a few girls from Girls' High. Some young guys on motorcycles decided to rev up their wheels in the middle of the night to attract the comely young American ladies they spotted through the window of the hotel.

The commotion woke a bunch of school kids from another Italian town, along with their chaperone, a wizened high school teacher who burst out of his room wearing old-fashioned Long
John jammies with a real nightcap that had a purple pom pom dangling from it. Rip Van Winkle could have been his brother.

The chaperone shouted that he'd told the manager to investigate our tour group for disturbing the peace and said he'd have the police throw us out. He called us "American rabble rousers," and said he'd read the book, *The Ugly American,* and that it was 100% true. In his view, we were totally ignorant of other cultures, and uncouth and disrespectful. When we protested, he screamed at us in Italian, so we figured it was best not to respond, since we didn't understand what he said anyway.

At that point, the hotel manager appeared on the scene to investigate the man's accusations. The chaperone was waving his hands wildly and cursing in Italian (I'd heard a few of those words growing up) as he presented his case. The manager put his hand on the chaperone's shoulder and said, "I will tell the intruders to leave immediately. I apologize for your trouble. Now, please return to your room, and everything will be fine."

The manager turned to me, "I am sorry for the disturbance. I understand that it was not your fault. I'll take care of everything. No worries," he said in perfect English.

We all parted amicably and went our separate ways. The manager was a true diplomat and handled us as Dad would have, so that in the end, everyone left peacefully and enjoyed the rest of their time at the hotel.

After I started working at Girls' High, Andrew got a call saying that due to a drop in the student population, he'd be transferred to another school in a neighborhood on the other end of town, not far from Rosa Parks High School, where I'd worked previously. He was only there for about a year and then opted to go back to the school in northeast Philly where we originally started. He knew many staff members there, so it was an easy adjustment.

The kids loved and respected Andrew, and he had great classroom control, even with the "derries," as Dad would have called the troublemakers, the hardest kids to handle. Andrew never had to say a word or threaten his students with phone calls home, detention, or a trip to the principal's office. He had a presence that no one could match.

After thirty plus years each in the system, we both decided to take an early retirement as the state passed a bill for teachers who taught a certain number of years so that they could retire with similar benefits than staying longer in the system would benefit them. The district wanted to give an incentive to older teachers in order to attract and pay less to younger ones starting out in the profession. That sounded good to me as I always wished for more time to write and practice the psychic arts. The souls in the Roosevelt Cemetery would approve, I was sure.

Chapter Eighteen
A New Life for the Lovebirds

"Let's get the hell out of here."
—me to Andrew in church.

Andrew and I embarked on our new life after we both taught a total of sixty-seven years in Philadelphia. I got a part-time job working as a student teaching supervisor and adjunct assistant professor at Temple, my alma mater. Dad always said that Penn, from which he graduated, was the best university, but I disagreed because of my memorable professors and good ethnic mix. Plus, the food trucks offered treats from every corner of the world. That was important for a commuter like me who couldn't spend much time on campus.

I loved going to different schools in the Bucks County suburbs observing and evaluating student teachers. I was surprised that most of them wanted to teach elementary school, but I wasn't concerned as a high school teacher about how to mentor them because no matter what grade level you taught, most of the issues you faced were the same, like how to control a class, how to teach the subject matter effectively, and how to get kids engaged in learning.

Most of the teachers I worked with decided to teach elementary school because they were put off by disciplining older kids whom they thought might intimidate them. I told them that their fears weren't necessarily valid because usually if the students both liked and respected you, classroom control would not be too difficult. Of course, this was not true in every case as some of the older students could be physically and psychologically intimidating, especially if they were taking drugs.

When I taught high school, I appreciated the fact that in high school principals were usually too busy to observe teachers excessively, which could shake up a teacher, and that you had a certain degree of autonomy following the curriculum by using your own unique teaching methods. Also, elementary education majors, who are also certified to teach middle school, had to pass proficiency tests in subjects other than their majors, while secondary teachers were required to show proficiency only in their major and minor subject areas.

Most of the student teachers I mentored stayed in their field of study and are still there today. I had only one student, Margo, who dropped out at the student teaching stage, a young woman who went to school with my daughter. She student-taught AP classes at the high school I graduated from and found disciplining the students difficult because the students constantly challenged her. I suggested library science as a possible new career path, and Margo was happy once she changed her major, even at this late stage. Mom used to say, "It's never too late to change your mind, and there's no disgrace in it." She was right in this case.

At around the same time, I also started writing books, a lifelong dream. My books dealt mainly with bullying because it was such a pervasive problem in the schools. My daughter Shayna, an educator herself, suggested the idea, and I ran with it, believing she was right. As a teacher and counselor, she'd seen many episodes of bullying and the devastation caused by it. I later branched out to writing about parenting, women's issues, and spirituality.

I found giving talks about my books in Ocean City every summer rewarding because I love helping writers find fulfillment from writing, whether they get paid or not. The give and take of an adult audience gave me the same fulfillment that teaching did. I guess deep down I was always "Catty School" and enjoyed that role to the max. I have Uncle Tony to thank for that as he was my first student and a good one at that.

After retiring, I also accelerated my psychic business, doing phone readings and teaching classes on different metaphysical arts. My friend in Ocean City invited me to read in her shop, "Blue Sky in the Morning," a fashionable boutique. I also did phone and in-person readings and loved doing readings at Rouget, a restaurant in Bucks County near my home.

Sometimes psychic readings can surprise the reader as well as the person being read. Once I gave a police officer a reading and experienced a strong pain in my neck area. Because my main psychic modality is psychic touch or clairsentience, I felt severe pain in the exact area of my body (my neck), where the officer suffered a gunshot wound.

Another surprising thing happened when I gave my friend Lucy a reading. I didn't think of myself as a psychic medium, but when I was reading Lucy's cards, I began to talk in the jerky, stilted manner that her dad spoke, and I gave her a message from him in words similar to those he'd use. She appreciated hearing from him that day, and I was happy to be the vehicle for putting her in touch with him.

The weirdest thing that happened when I did psychic work involved Rocco, a middle-aged man, who came to see me because he was concerned that someone (he knew the alleged culprit) had put a curse on his mother's house. He asked me to take the curse away. Since I don't think of myself as an exorcist or a witch doctor, I politely declined.

Rocco vigorously persisted, so I suggested that he visit a priest who could perform a ritual, sprinkling holy water on his mom and her house to take the curse away. He said he'd consult a visiting priest to his parish who didn't know Rocco well. As brazen as Rocco was, I sensed he was embarrassed. I hoped that Rocco didn't disclose my identity, or the priest might have doomed me to hellfire for setting him up with Rocco. Rocco thought about talking to the priest for a moment and said he'd try it and went happily on his way to the rectory.

The next Sunday I attended Mass at the local church where the visiting priest that Rocco consulted helped out the parish by conducting additional masses for the busy summer season. I was shocked when I saw an usher walk down the aisle with his basket to collect money for the Sunday donation. I was nearly face to face with no other than Rocco, the man who'd asked me to remove the curse from his mother's house. I thought quickly and told Andrew we had to leave church immediately before Rocco spotted me.

Andrew frowned at me during the sermon. "We have to leave now before the service is over? I don't know if I can walk out of here with the entire congregation staring at me and wondering what's wrong," he said. "I say we wait until they say the Profession of Faith, so it doesn't look so obvious," he added.

"Let's get the hell out of here now," I said louder than I should have.

The elderly couple next to me gave out a hearty laugh.

"I don't want that usher to see me," I said. "I'll explain later. Just get your ass out of this pew before I jump over you and leave by myself."

Andrew knew I meant business, and we both race-walked out of the church, leaving Rocco six comfortable pews behind. He looked so innocent with his usher's white jacket and plaid bow tie that he could have been an altar boy. Little did the priest or congregation know that he was sinning against the first commandment, "Thou shalt not put strange gods before me," by going to a psychic and that I had sinned grievously also, possibly damning us both to the eternal flames.

I guess Rocco pestered the poor priest until he couldn't take it anymore (shades of Uncle Tony bothering Father O'Loughlin in the confessional about *relsteen*, his magic word), so that Father, the same priest I saw at Mass that day, agreed and said some prayers over the house for Rocco's Mom. That didn't satisfy Rocco, though.

The following week Rocco came back to my friend's shop to ask me for another reading to verify that the curse on his mother was truly gone. I told him that it's best not to have too many readings in a short time. I knew that many of the same ideas may come through if the next reading comes too soon after the one before. I didn't want Rocco to waste his money, and besides, he drove me to distraction. I didn't tell him that part, but he wouldn't have listened anyway. He protested, and I emphatically told him I wouldn't read for him again. He'd be better off seeing another psychic at a later date.

The spirits in Roosevelt Cemetery would have been happy. I listened when they spoke and found satisfaction in exploring the ever after, the unseen world. In my previous jobs and in all other aspects of my life, I depended on my psychic senses to guide me in advising people, but I didn't let on to anyone other than friends and family that I was using these abilities. My employers may not have looked upon these talents favorably, especially people of certain religious proclivities.

Earlier in this book, I pointed out that Jesus used His supernatural abilities to help his followers. I don't see any problem with it unless you have a narrow view of religion and its precepts. Using psychic abilities to help myself and others has enhanced my life and brought me immeasurable satisfaction.

During this time, Andrew and I spent summers at the seashore, our favorite place. He found time to do the things he was always too busy to do, like ride his bike on the boardwalk and eat Browns' donuts at the little coffee shop on the boardwalk, which made him sublimely happy. Lacking the stresses that hectic schedules brought to our lives, we were able to handle our conflicts more peaceably, and found ourselves different now from the way some people at Penndel Court Apartments described us: "They're a nice couple, but all they do is fight." Of course, we still had disagreements, but we tried our best to manage them.

Then, wham-o, Shingles struck. I woke up three years ago with an itchy, bitchy rash that dogged me day and night. We were at the seashore but forget the beach and boardwalk. Every day I lay on the sofa in my pajamas, unable to join in the fun. Andrew kept my spirits up by taking me to my favorite eateries even though food turned me off. He wiped my tears when I complained how crappy I felt and couldn't rouse myself from the couch. He rubbed my back to lessen the pain of every nerve and muscle.

I learned during my virulent bout with Shingles how important Andrew was to me and decided that I wasn't going to waste too much time (well, maybe a little), arguing with him. I also believe that fighting isn't necessarily a bad thing. For some people like us, I think it can act as a catalyst for helping them work things out so they can stay together. These days, our arguments usually lead to a resolution, but without the fight, we may not get there.

It's pleasing to note that we've come full circle. We now find joy every day in one another's presence and tolerate each other's idiosyncrasies and foibles as we never did when we worked one or more jobs and attended graduate school, along with carrying out our parenting duties. That's not to say we don't ever have disagreements, but when we do, we go back to Dear Abby's question: "Would I be better off with or without them?" The answer for both of us is always a resounding *with*.

Now that we're senior retired people, we have more challenges and decisions ahead of us. Health issues have slowed us down a bit but have not stopped us from enjoying our lives to the fullest. Our kids are grown, and we have grandchildren, ranging in age from twelve to twenty-three. We keep in touch with them and learn from them, along with passing on our ancestral wisdom, or we'd like to imagine we do. We try to guide them along their individual paths but don't preach or pontificate. As Mom and Dad did, we tell them what we think but encourage them to make their own decisions and choices in life.

We're also grappling with the idea of leaving our home, which we've lived in for years, and moving to a community. It won't be like our first apartment, where everyone knew everyone else's business and banged on our ceiling for silence with a broom handle when our arguments got too loud. Hopefully, someone like "Big Boy" won't lurk outside our door.

It's a challenge getting older and having all these decisions to make, but living at The Royal Gardens gave me a sense of adventure and taught me to appreciate different types of people
and situations. It showed me the necessity of taking things as they come. It also taught me the importance of having a thick skin and showing resilience. It definitely isn't easy, but considering the alternative, it's the only way to go.

Chapter Nineteen
Theresa, the Little Flower

"Mom called Theresa her pride and joy. Theresa would joke about it when she got older and call herself 'PJ' or a funny word she coined, 'Poopie Joop.'"

When I was a junior in high school, my parents started listening to Dad's psychiatrist, who always swore that their problem was Mom's lack of interest in sex. My parents must have finally paid attention this time and revived their love life, or at least it seemed that way to me. Mom got pregnant, but none of us could tell, except for Dad, who already knew.

Mom was on the heavy side, so she didn't begin to show until her seventh month. When she started wearing Dad's baggy flannel shirts and conked out at eight before our scary radio shows hit the airwaves, I knew something was up—but pregnant at her age? Surprise, surprise!

When I found out, I couldn't believe that she and Dad did stuff to make a baby. They were old, for God's sake. My friends were equally shocked and could never imagine their parents having a love life. I was doubly surprised since Dad still said mean things to her, made her cry, and didn't appreciate everything she did for him, like ironing his droopy boxer shorts and torn undershirts, and serving him his favorite foods, like barbequed pork chops and potatoes and eggs on Fridays when eating meat was forbidden to Catholics.

On Fridays we never ate meat since we were good Catholics. Priests from Our Lady of Grace, like Monsignor Clark and Father Houlihan, loved to eat dinner at our new house. Dad and Mom started them out with a tall glass of Chianti and gave them three-course dinners like their favorite Italian dishes or prime rib with roasted potatoes. They were so happy to get away from the cook at the rectory who made dinners like boiled hot dogs and gassy baked beans three times a week. The priests must have kept a lot of Gas-Ex in their medicine chest so they wouldn't offend the parishioners. The franks were limp and tasteless, not like Cliff's greasy French fried hot dogs that stuck to your ribs. The cook at the rectory dressed like my Aunt Minnie with a drab housedress and had false teeth like her too, but I guess that's the only kind of cook they could afford.

I was so excited about the baby that I asked Dad and Mom if I could name her. If it was a girl, which I knew psychically it would be, I wanted to name her Leilani, which means heavenly flower in Hawaiian. The spirits at the Roosevelt cemetery finally started sending me messages again and told me it would fit her to a tee, and I thought so too. I was thrilled when my parents agreed that it would be a perfect name, and yes, I could name the baby.

At the beginning of December, my parents had lined up Newt Jones, our neighbor, across the street to drive Mom to the hospital since an icy week was forecast. Mr. Jones attached chains to his trusty jeep and plowed through the snow to drive Mom to Abington Hospital to have her baby. The baby had dark brown eyes that took up most of her rosy oval face like a Keane painting and light brown hair with a widow's peak just like Mom's.

When I saw my sister for the first time, I couldn't believe how beautiful she looked. She was born smiling and never stopped smiling for ever after. My high school friends lined up at our front door for their chance to see her laughing and cooing in her pink bassinette in the family room. They all looked so jealous.

Oh, and guess what? My parents changed their minds about my naming the baby. Instead of Leilani, they named her Theresa, after St. Therese of Lisieux who people call The Little Flower because if you pray to her with all your heart, she'll send you pictures of flowers or real flowers, or even better, let flowers fall from the heavens.

St. Theresa was also a famous doctor of the church. That must have pissed off the priests big time because she was a woman. I was sad about not being about to name my sister, but I saw after a few weeks that the name Theresa started to fit her, so I shut up about it, which made my parents happy because I could be a total nag when I wanted to.

Mom and I loved taking care of Theresa and were thrilled when she'd smile at us and babbled in her sweet little voice. Dad was a different story. He couldn't stand the fact that Mom was giving the baby so much attention and didn't give in to all his demands, like having dinner on the table at 5:00 PM sharp or not laying out his clothes before he returned to work at night. He would never admit he was jealous of a little baby, but he showed it in his actions by sulking around the house or looking grumpy.

Although he missed all the attention Mom gave him before the baby's arrival, he loved Theresa and made up a song up for her, where he called her "Theresa Nella, Nella, Nella" that he sang in his croaky, off-key voice. He bought her doll babies that cried and peed and special pastries from Neffle's Bakery, like elephant ears and creamy cakes that oozed butter. She was his princess.

Mom called Theresa her pride and joy. Theresa would joke about it when she got older and call herself "PJ" or "Poopie Joop," and we'd all laugh. Theresa never took Dad and Mom's
special feelings for her as the baby of the family seriously or let it go to her head and didn't want to see Joe or me feel slighted or left out.

Eventually, Dad got over his feelings of playing second fiddle to the baby and often held Theresa to quiet her down during her fussy hour, which never lasted more than fifteen minutes. "Theresa Nella, Nella, Nella," he'd sing and strut around the room with her, patting her on the back until her fierce cries died down.

However, his insatiable need for attention was probably one reason he started an affair with Ada, the disgusting lady in the housing complex in back of the bar. Mom almost divorced him over it. When she found out about the affair from a phone call from Ada herself, Mom took off for Baltimore like she did when I was a baby but returned home after a weekend to her house on Azalea Lane. She and Dad acted as if nothing happened, and they never mentioned it again. They stayed together for the rest of their lives.

I carried the lessons I learned at The Royal Gardens over to our home at 505 Azalea Lane. One thing I figured out is how hard it is for people to change. Take Dad, for instance. All those years of going to therapists at the mental health center didn't make him much different from how I've always remembered him. I'd hate to think about how he would have ended up if he hadn't talked with those doctors about his problems. That's not to say that people can't change, because I believe they can if they set their minds to it and get the right help, but it isn't easy and didn't happen much in our case.

Dad dragged his demons around until the end, and everyone around him bore the brunt of it, especially Mom. Maybe if she'd left him earlier, things would have been different, but Mom believed what the Catholic Church teaches, that marriage is forever, "til death do us part," no matter what.

In some ways staying together served both of them well. Dad couldn't have made it without Mom's strength and support, and she couldn't have been happy without having him around, despite his mood swings and bossy ways. I guess you learn to need and like what you get used to. We kids were often ripped apart by the way my parents dealt with each other, but now I'm glad they stayed together because I think that was what they wanted.

We loved both of them despite the drama, tears and chaos that often marked our days. I'm not saying there weren't good times too, like when Dad took us to the Penn relay races or baseball games, or treated us to a special dinner at a fancy restaurant for Mom's birthday.

For Christmas, he'd always get her fancy nightgowns with silk and lace, and she'd *ooh* and *ahh* over them like she was seeing them for the first time, even though he'd bought something similar at the same shop the year before. But that was the way it was. It worked because we made it work. We were all in it together, and we stayed together no matter what. I wonder if there's something to be said for that.

Chapter Twenty
There is No One in this World Like Theresa.

"My heart leaps up when I behold a rainbow in the sky."
—William Wordsworth

Because we were older when Theresa was born, my husband and I always thought of my sister as a daughter. We took her everywhere we went, along with our own kids, for barge rides in New Hope, car trips to the Jersey shore, Florida beaches, and to New Haven, where my in-laws ran a laundry business, and my husband spent his childhood days.

There she met my husband's mother, Grandma Rose, his father, Grandpa Pete, his brother, Anthony, and his charming wife, Dotti, and her three cousins, Rosanne, Angela, and Lisa. Theresa made herself at home wherever we took her. Everyone wanted her to stay longer because she was fun to be around, joking and laughing, and willing to help out. She was always up, never down, no matter what life threw her way.

When she was a little girl, Uncle Tony gave her one of his expensive white chocolate Easter baskets, stuffed with chocolate eggs, jellybeans in rainbow colors, and milk chocolate bunnies. As always, Theresa told him how thankful she was for the special gifts he gave her. Aunt Mary was another story, but Theresa always reached out to her with love and affection, no matter how outrageous she acted.

Aunt Mary sometimes called us from Linwood, New Jersey (She always started by saying, "This is Aunt Mary from Linwood") and erupted into long monologues about her prior students, what she was eating that night, and what she planned to eat at Mac's restaurant (the lasagna or the fish of the day) when she and her husband Josh went for their weekly date night.

To get off the phone, I sometimes made excuses like, "I have to mark papers" or "make dinner" when dinner was only a frozen pizza, which took no time at all to pop in the oven and sprinkle with grated Parmesan. You couldn't stop the conversation when you talked to Aunt Mary, but Theresa knew how to respond to her without hurting her feelings. On the other hand, I felt trapped by those long phone calls, and my blood pressure shot up 100 points; I wondered how I could control a rowdy high school class and not deal with my elderly aunt's interminable phone talks.

Sometime after Mom moved into Green Valley, Theresa and I called Aunt Mary out of concern and because we hadn't heard from her for months. Mom once remarked how distant Mary had been to her since she'd moved to the independent living facility. She couldn't figure out why since they'd gotten along pretty well, except for the time Dad told Mary not to visit him when he was in the hospital during his final illness. She went anyway, and she got all huffy and stormed out of his hospital room.

Dad didn't tell her that he couldn't stand her state of perpetual agitation and constant fussing over him, but that was the way she was, and I don't believe she could help it. Mom told Mary that dad didn't want visitors because he was tired, but once when she saw her sister Minnie coming out of Dad's hospital room, she put on a show for the nurses and threw a tantrum.

"Why is Minnie here?" she asked. "I thought he didn't want visitors, or does that only apply to me? Now I know how all of you really feel about me. You won't see me or hear from me again." And she never returned.

That was the last time that Mom or any of us heard from Aunt Mary. We think it may have had more to do with Mom going into independent living in Green Valley than Dad's telling her not to visit him. Maybe Mary thought that if she talked to Mom or any of us about going into what she called "the old people's home," she might end up there too. Who could figure out why she acted the way she did? Least of all, me.

Theresa was always the diplomat, trying to get everyone on the same page, as she was when we tried to call Aunt Mary that final time. Besides knowing how to deal with people, Theresa excelled in all subjects in high school, but her specialty was science. She also had a photographic memory that made all school subjects easy for her to learn. She didn't have to spend hours studying for tests like most kids.

Her ready smile and willingness to help her fellow-students endeared teachers to her and made her popularity in school soar. I admired her and her desire to live in harmony with all the other students from diverse assortments of different high school groups. Even girls in the snobby clique loved her and invited her to join in their activities although she politely declined.

Theresa worked at numerous fast food and all-you-can eat joints, as many teenagers do, to get spending money. Boys flocked to Theresa, and after "Gunga Dean" departed from the scene, a slew of boys knocked at her door in Azalea Lane. Much to Dad's chagrin, Dean, her first beau, delighted in setting up a small truck-farming business with locally grown produce in a choice parking spot (depriving other patrons of parking there) outside The Royal Gardens. Dean's business flourished until he got tired of doing all the work connected with selling produce out of a ramshackle red pick-up truck at the bar.

My sister, who had a strong work ethic, finally realized that Dean wasn't for her. Like many kids, Theresa liked having a drink or two with her girlfriends after work until Mom ordered her to stop being a wild party girl and stick around the house a little more. Theresa yessed Mom to death but did her own thing. She ended up fine even though she came home from a couple of her jaunts feeling mighty happy. She had the sense to never drive after she had a few drinks and made sure her friends didn't either. My sister always had good common sense.

Theresa landed her first job as a cytogenetic technologist immediately after graduating from Villanova University. She often said how much she enjoyed her job, except for one part: visiting patients to take their blood to determine the current status of their leukemia. Some of the patients were very young, and it saddened Theresa to realize that a few would die from their illness. When she married John, she quit her job to become a full-time homemaker and raise five sons.

She moved to Reading, PA, and later to a farm in nearby Oley, where she raised organic fruits and vegetables that graced her own table and those of neighbors. She never considered herself mainly a housewife, though. She loved having her own interests and ways of making money of her own.

Theresa made delicious dishes for a local organic catering business and hosted many parties for family and friends. She catered business functions for her husband John's medical practice and showcased her culinary skills for the catering company by cooking and baking her specialties. She excelled in making American foods and many ethnic foods, traditional dishes with a gourmet twist, and turned out artistically decorated cookies and exotic pies and cakes that tasted as good as they looked.

My sister kept physically fit by exercising vigorously and becoming a role model of skill and stamina for the ladies in her neighborhood who attended aerobic and step classes. She volunteered in the local soup kitchen and senior center, making elaborate breakfasts for those in the program.

My pet name for her throughout the years was Theresa Cat, and she called me Catto because I love cats and went to Catholic School. After Mom died, Theresa became the matriarch of our family, cooking lavish family dinners and helping solve problems that came up in our growing families. If you have someone like her in your family, consider yourself blessed.

Her sons grew into exemplary young men. Two worked in the medical field and loved to give their patients personal attention; one exceled in business and made the best macadamia nut cookies, and two worked in the hospitality industry where they made all their guests feel at home when they're far from home.

Best of all, they are all loving human beings like their mom, always willing to help others. They have their mom's ready smile and desire to go the extra mile for the people they serve. They now have families of their own and continue the tradition of teaching their kids the virtues and the importance of maintaining a sense of service and integrity.

Theresa spent time working for a man who owned a popular Italian restaurant near her Oley farm. She helped transform the restaurant into a hot spot by cooking fresh chicken from her farm rather than the frozen patties the cook used before she appeared on the scene. She also baked specialty desserts, like chocolate silk pie and cookies with multicolored sprinkles.

Finally, Theresa landed her dream job, creating culinary delights for an organic food store in Oley, a town near Reading, Pennsylvania. Locals swooped up her wares so there were none left when the next person appeared at the door. Talk about supply and demand. People swarmed to the shop the way they loved to frequent The Royal Gardens for Mom's banquet fare of prime rib and roast turkey, not to mention those decadent banana cream pies and peach cobblers. It was the same with Theresa. You couldn't beat her cooking skills.

Now that her kids were grown and starting new careers, Theresa was free to do whatever she wanted to, to go where she wanted, and to use her creative cooking skills to build a new career, possibly her own catering business. She would live happily ever after, dreaming of a storybook future, which included being "Granny," (what my kids called my mom and the name she chose for herself) to her grandkids with more on the way.

Then suddenly, out of the blue, when she was out and about, Theresa bumped her head. The bump felt uncomfortable, but she thought it was nothing serious, so she visited her doctor for a physical, just in case.

Since it was a head injury, the doctor checked her out for a concussion, which it wasn't, and sent her to an ophthalmologist to do further studies. That's when they discovered she had ocular melanoma, a rare cancer that settled in her eye. We were all in shock, and we prayed to Padre Pio, all the angels and saints, St. Jude, the Patron Saint of the Impossible, and Blessed Carlos Acutis, a young Italian techie, who needed one more miracle to become a saint. I guess God had other plans for her.

The ophthalmologist immediately referred Theresa to a top oncologist, who recommended chemotherapy. Her veins couldn't tolerate the treatment, so doctors tried radiation, which helped for a while. When they discovered that the cancer had spread to her liver, as it does in a high percentage of cases of ocular melanoma. She was willing to try an experimental treatment, but the oncologist looked into it and told her that it wouldn't help and might make things worse, so after two years of living with the illness and having treatments, she chose to go into hospice care. Throughout this time, she said she was at peace and coped with her illness with faith and courage, as Mom had faced all her marital and health problems throughout the years.

For the few weeks of her life, my daughters, Melissa and Lauren, stayed at an Airbnb near her home to be by her side and help things go smoothly at home. All her children and grandkids, Joe and I showed up for her during her last days.

Theresa reassured my daughters that she felt at peace and told them her last wishes for her service. She wanted to be cremated and then have a small gathering of family and friends meet at a pleasant eatery where they served good food. Before mourners left the restaurant, Lauren sang "Landslide" by Fleetwood MAC, accompanied by John, Theresa's husband, on guitar, along with Drew and Luke, my grandsons.

When Joe and I visited our sister for the last time, I gave her a Reiki treatment. My daughter Shayna said that she saw Mom in the bedroom where we did the treatment and that her presence was palpable and strong. From what I'd experienced with Mom seeing Dad shortly before her death, I knew that my sister's time on this earth was drawing to a close.

Theresa was sleeping on the sofa when we left her for the last time to go back to Bucks County. Joe went to get the car, and she woke up briefly to give me one of her famous fierce hugs. "I'll see you again," she said, her large eyes taking me in fully, and then she lapsed into a peaceful sleep. She also told Missy and Lauren shortly before she died that she'd see them again. I believe she meant it. Joe and I made plans to make the trip to Theresa's house the following week.

A couple of days later, Lauren left the house to return to the Airbnb at 1:00 AM. Missy settled next to Theresa in her bedroom. Her husband John was also in the room, sitting in a chair, keeping watch. On February 1, she died peacefully at 3:00 AM. Her boys came in to say goodbye, and it was a tearful leave-taking, according to all present.

None of us could believe she was gone. We held out hope for her until the end. I remember joking with her that "It ain't over until the fat lady sings," which was one of Mom's favorite sayings, meaning "Never give up."

Today, a couple of years later, we still can't fathom it. The memorial service was meaningful and moving, planned by Missy and Lauren, just the way Theresa wanted it. Hundreds of family and friends flowed into the funeral home, where my sister's ashes sat in an alcove for all to pay their final respects to a lady they said wore a perpetual smile and made fast friends with everyone she met.

Melissa and Lauren posted videos and pictures of Theresa taken throughout the years, Theresa smiling, laughing, cooking Sunday dinner all the days of the year, hiking, riding a surrey with the grandkids, doing the things she loved best with those she loved.

The room wreaked of the cloying smell of flowers, and I felt myself becoming dizzy. When Theresa's husband John gave me the signal, I felt my energy return, and I went up to the mic and read my birthday poem to Theresa. Then I read "Sea Fever" by John Masefield because she loved the sea. The poem ends this way:

I must go down to the sea again, to the vagrant gypsy life.

To the gull's way and the whale's way where the wind's like a whetted knife.

And all I ask is a merry yarn from a laughing fellow-rover,

And quiet sleep and a sweet dream when the long trick's over.

At the end of the service, my daughters and I approached the alcove that contained the urn with my sister's ashes. We looked at each other for a long moment and held hands, and then I listened for a sign from Theresa. Everything and everyone else in the room seemed to disappear. I felt like I was totally alone in the room and was in Theresa's presence, which was strong and palpable, yet as light as air.

I suddenly felt my heart expand until I thought it was about to break open. And then the words entered my mind: "My heart leaps up when I behold a rainbow in the sky…" William Wordsworth, a romantic poet, wrote these words. The feeling and the words that rushed into my heart came to me unexpectedly, out of the ether, when I needed them most.

One afternoon when I was relaxing at home alone with a good book, I believe Theresa gave me a message. I knew how all of us were trying to survive without her; in many cases, it didn't seem to be working. It was gut-wrenchingly painful, but I wondered how she was getting along without all of us, especially her kids and grandkids. I needed to know.

Then the thought came into my mind. I could hear and sense her saying clearly that time is different where she is now. It will only be a millisecond until we see each other again—the blink of an eye. Time is happening simultaneously; past, present, and future are all the same. I believed this message and felt consoled that she would be okay. I felt it in the depths of my soul.

If I learned anything growing up in the Royal Gardens, I learned that there is an ever after where I'll meet the people who went before, the people I loved and who loved me on this earth, even Dr. Alex, Mr. Galeki, and all

Dad's cronies and my pets, Suzy Gray and Skipper, but most of all, Mom, Dad, and Theresa. It's not because I read it in The Baltimore Catechism or in a scientific journal that requires proof. I just know. Do you just know some things too?

Chapter Twenty-One
Ever, Ever After

"Sometimes, I feel the grief as if it just happened, sometimes I'm able to do the things I've always loved..."
— me, thinking about Theresa

After Theresa died, I felt grief-stricken for a long time and found it hard to live my life the way I used to. I couldn't seem to wrap my mind around the fact that she was gone and that I'd never see her again, at least in this life. Although I got signs from the spirit world that she was alive in the spirit world and still with us, only in another form, I feel sad that she's no longer with me to call me on the phone to say, "Hi, Catto, it's Theresa," or to let me know her latest travel plans, or what's going on with her boys, their wives, and the grandkids. They just presented her with two new granddaughters.

In search of finding some sense of peace in dealing with my sorrow over my sister's entrance into a new life that did not include me or any family members, I sought help but got turned away by every mental health professional. They told me that they were totally booked up because many people suffered from emotional problems due to Covid. They had trouble accommodating the patients they already had and could not see anyone else for a long time. They said they'd call if any opening came, but they never did.

One day I saw an ad on social media for a therapy venue that catered mainly to seniors. I took a chance and called the number. A friendly voice answered, and I made an appointment to talk to a clinical psychologist about my feelings of unrelenting grief and inability to get past it enough to get back to a semblance of who I once was.

An understanding therapist gave me practical suggestions and articles to read about what I was going through. I told him that I planned to write a letter to Theresa, telling her how I felt about her and missed her. I also decided to write one for Dad and Mom, in hopes that I'd be more in touch with their spirits, something like how I was able to communicate with the spirits in Roosevelt Cemetery.

I remember what the spirits in the Roosevelt Cemetery said to me when I was growing up: "Don't be sad for us. Things are better where we are now and much easier, so don't be afraid of life, death, and ever after. It's all good." That brought me solace and consolation. Maybe writing these letters would too. It was worth a try.

I believed what the spirits said, and I embraced their advice. Writing the letters helped and brought me to an understanding of how I felt about these three people who had strongly influenced my life. I feel better now having thought about what Dad, Mom, and Theresa mean to me and how much they still influence my life, but I will never forget them and still miss them each day.

The therapist told me that because Theresa not only took on the role of my sister but that she was also like a child to me and Andrew, we formed an unbreakable bond, and it would be harder for me to heal and to face my life again in the same way I did before I lost her. He was right. That double whammy socked me hard.

Sometimes, I feel the grief as if it just happened, sometimes I'm able to do the things I've always loved, like writing and psychic work. But then those precious memories creep into my mind, like the time at the shore that Theresa made Sunday dinner for all of us, laughing, joking, and drinking red wine, or the time she hiked miles on the Ocean City Beach with Joe, or went out deep in the sparkly waters, paddle boarding while in Hawaii with Missy and Lauren.

Appendix 1
Letters

Here are my letters to those I've loved and lost. I hope you write letters to those you've loved who have passed on. I think you'll find it therapeutic and comforting to share your thoughts about your past relationship and how you hope the present will turn out now that you've told them how you feel.

Letter to Dad

Dear Dad, AKA. "Joe the Bartender,"

I'm older, and maybe a little wiser now, than when you died, so it's given me a lot of time to think about the problems Mom and I faced dealing with your mental illness. I don't blame you for it although at the time, I thought you could control it, at least more than you did, so we could relate to one another as a "normal" family, whatever that is. Mom wouldn't have been on edge all the time, and you two would have gotten along much better. We could have shared more time planting trees and flowers, and you and I could have enjoyed more peaceful relaxing times playing with our pets and hanging out. But that's all in the past now, and I have to move forward.

Thank you for all you taught me about the beauty of languages and literature, the meanings and melodies of words, about looking up words in the big dictionary you kept on the shelf in the living room,. I appreciate what you taught me about love and loyalty among family members, even though Aunt Mary was a little out of it and Uncle Tony made up weird words and kept the math lessons I taught him in his desk drawer, along with his Fig Newtons. I think most people have a few unusual relatives, but I believe we can learn something from all of our family members, no matter how strange and quirky they might appear to others.

You had a strong, abiding simple faith in God and enjoyed going to High Mass with all its singing and pageantry. You loved singing "Holy God, We Praise Thy Name" louder than all the people at Church even though you had a terrible voice. Another thing that ticked me off was how you used to park in the grocery store parking lot that was far from Our Lady of Grace Church, and we had to trudge to the church even in the rain and snow. The older you got, the farther away you parked, so your beloved Chrysler wouldn't get scratched up. But that was all okay. It seems like such a small thing now. At least we got some exercise.

You were a learned scholar, but like a little child when it came to religion. Wasn't it Jesus who said, "Truly I tell you, anyone who does not receive the kingdom of God like a little child will never enter it."? Pretty heavy stuff.

I remember when you were very sick you said, "I just want to feel like my old self again." My wish is that you do now and that all the mental and physical turmoil you suffered has disappeared and that you are whole and functioning beautifully.

So, I want to tell you, Dad, that I love you and appreciate you and how you helped mold me into who I am today. I still prefer Temple University's cherry and white to the University of Pennsylvania's red and blue, and I would still tell that roughneck in the bar off again if I had the chance, despite your telling me to shut up or he might beat you up. I forgive you for anything hurtful you said or did as I hope you forgive me.

Your daughter,
Cathy, AKA Cassie

Letter to Mom

Dear Mom AKA Grace, Mary Grace, Maria Grazia,

I was shocked and saddened to lose you. I thought you'd have a few more good years to enjoy your life once you moved to Green Valley Retirement Village. If anyone deserved those years, you did after how deeply you loved all of us, how hard you worked, and how much we needed you to be around.

So many times, I got angry when you didn't stand up for yourself when Dad gave you a rough time, bossed you around, or said terrible things to you, but I realize that women of your generation didn't learn assertiveness skills when they were growing up.

As the years went by, you became more independent and stood your ground when Dad or anyone else tried to take advantage of you. I remember the day when you announced to all of us that "the worm has turned." That meant you weren't going to tolerate any type of mistreatment anymore. You stuck by your word and turned into a strong woman, I would call you a feminist, always with a gentle touch. You never lost that.

You taught me so many things throughout the years; for instance, the importance of finding something you love to do in life—in my case teaching, writing, and psychic work. You helped me hone practical skills, such as being an advocate for myself and others when we interact with doctors and other professionals, how to negotiate and not be taken advantage when dealing with businesses, and how to cook and manage money.

I wasn't interested in cooking or any of the domestic arts when I was growing up, but later I watched you cook and learned how to prepare many of your famous recipes, which were surprisingly easy to prepare and always magnificent. I particularly loved your Italian dishes, like lasagna made with crushed meatballs rather than ground beef, and your strawberry shortcake made with real whipped cream.

You read to me every day and turned me into a voracious reader and lover of all types of literature. You were smarter with a high school degree than many grad students I knew. You taught me the importance of being a good listener and how to be there for others when they need me most, how to make eye contact and simply listen without adding my two cents or judgments. Most of all, you taught me to cherish my family and make them the most important people in my life.

Mom, I will love you forever, remember everything you taught me, and try my best to live up to your expectations of me.

Your daughter,
Catherine Louise, AKA Cath

Letter to Theresa

Dear Theresa Cat,

I'm writing to say I love you and I miss you in so many ways. I miss talking to you on the phone and hearing your messages. I've saved them all. I love when you said "Hi, Catto, it's Theresa" or simply, "Catto" with the stress on the first syllable. I miss your telling me what's happening with your sons, Matt, Luke, Steve, Johnnie, and Mikey, and, of course, the grandkids and all the new ones you're going to meet that are born this year and ever after.

I believe you can see everyone and that you attend family get togethers. You're with us still. Maybe you're in the presence of angels and saints, maybe you're reincarnated, possibly you're helping out little kids who have just crossed over, as a psychic medium said recently. I have no idea where you are, but I feel your presence every day, all day long.

I hear you telling me not to worry about stuff like health or Andrew and how we'll ride the rough waves of life. "It will all work out," you always said, "Wait and see," even when you went into hospice care when the cancer couldn't be treated anymore, even with immunotherapy.

I'll never forget that night you sent me a sign I asked for. Your pet name that Mom called you was (pride and joy). You shortened it to PJ and then made up Poopie Joop (you were always making up silly words) to make fun of it all so Joe and I wouldn't get hurt feelings. You always thought of how other people felt, and you wanted them to feel good. You know how I always watched Sixers basketball. That night your name for yourself, *PJ*, flashed across the screen, and I jumped up and cheered, "My sign!" After the beer commercial, the announcer later explained that he was referring to a player, PJ Tucker, but I knew you had sent the sign just for me. Thanks for that.

You also said that we'll meet again. You said these things with true conviction and with a smile wide as the sky. I'll never forget that smile, or your faith and fortitude throughout your life, especially during your fight with ocular melanoma. I'll always remember how you gave the hospice workers tea and homemade cookies the day before you died, acting like dying was a perfectly natural process. They couldn't believe when they heard you'd died, after as you seemed so alive and alert the day before, taking a shower, styling your hair, and applying make-up as you did every day to look your best. Mom always said how important that was.

I was with you from the beginning when Mom and Dad brought you home from the hospital, and throughout the years our relationship turned into a warm and lasting friendship. I never thought you'd leave us so soon. I pictured you seeing all your boys marry, having many amazing grandkids (you already had four) that looked so much like you, and starting your own catering business, which was one of your goals. You were talented academically and taught us all so many of your practical skills like cooking.

You were always Martha Stewart, and I was a bookworm and career person, but we shared our lives with each other. You taught me how to live and die, and I taught you psychic things like how to connect with your angels and the magic of Reiki healing.

Thanks, Theresa Cat, for being my sister and my friend. We'll all be together one day. I know that in my heart. Until we meet again…

Your loving sister,
Catto

Appendix 2
Family Quotes

Here are some family quotes that we've heard over the years. Some of them will make perfect sense to you, while others may leave you scratching your head, but that's okay. Every family has their own secret codes that immediately conjure up certain emotions and some of these are ours. We relate to them as you relate to yours and gain meaning and memories from them.

Never forget your unique family quotes, even if initially they sound like the clichés of old because they'll bring back memories and maybe mean more to you now than they did when your family used to say them as part of the soundtrack of your life. Think of compiling a list of them as a keepsake for your family to hand down to the generations.

Family Quotes We Know and Love

"Let everything go over the bridge." This is my favorite quote from Mom. She said it when one of her family members suffered emotionally or experienced problems in their lives. Mother Catlin, an elderly border at my grandmother Carmella's house, originally said it. Everyone called her *mother* as a symbol of respect and because she was everyone in the family's mom.

Mother Catlin experienced a hard life when her husband left her for another woman, but she prevailed because she was strong and resilient, like Mom. She and Mom never let life's circumstances get the better of them, and they both came out winners. When things went wrong at our house, Mom made us one of her home-cooked dinners and said, "Let everything go over the bridge." Those words helped us heal, no matter what happened.

"Do nothing before you do anything." Richard Robinson, my

department head at Lincoln High School, said this. I think and say it often because it works. It's best not to jump into doing something when you're not sure of what to do to remedy a problem. Think it over and consider whether you're approaching your situation from the correct angle before you leap into something that may make things worse. In other words, think about what to do, instead of reacting. Don't rush into things.

"It ain't over 'til the fat lady sings": This was originally said by Texas sports director Ralph Carpenter. Mom and I sometimes quoted it without paying deference to political incorrectness. It means that we shouldn't presume anything about the outcome of an event which still hasn't yet played out. Things can change at any moment, and we never know how things will turn out in the end. When I said this to my sister Theresa toward the end of her life, she gave me one of her famous smiles. I believe that she always held out hope, I know I did, even when there was no longer hope. It helped keep her and me going despite the physical and emotional pain she endured, always with courage.

"Don't pamper yourself": Mom always said this, which is the opposite of most psychologists' advice, especially when you're going through hard times, or you feel terrible about something. Keep your chin up and face your problem head-on with strength and courage is what she'd say. Don't wallow in your misery and give yourself the luxury of feeling sorry for yourself. You can get through your problem if you're willing to move forward.

"What, me worry?" was one of Dad's favorite sayings. Alfred E. Neuman, the gap-toothed young man on the cover of *Mad Magazine* personified this expression that meant it doesn't pay to worry. Rather, it's important to show confidence and not be pulled down by the negative blows' life deals us. What did Dad have in common with this saying he loved? For one thing, he resembled Alfred E. Newman in that he had a missing tooth, but he hid it with a false tooth that he removed with his tongue when he said Alfred's favorite saying, so he'd have a gap tooth like the *Mad Magazine* hero.

Neumann always displayed that gap in his upper mouth, while Dad's showed off the gap in his lower mouth. Dad hated worrying and tried his best to stop doing it, but unlike Alfred, he couldn't stop it; however, he always presented an image of confidence and camaraderie to his customers who knew and loved him, unlike the man we knew who constantly battled his anxieties and insecurities. In his own way, he represented a winner who projected confidence. What, me worry?

"Some of these days you're gonna miss me, honey…" Mom often sang the words to this song that Sophie Tucker, and in later years, Ella Fitzgerald recorded. Listen to one of their u-tube videos to catch the lyrics. You may think that Mom was trying to lay a guilt trip on us by singing these lyrics, I don't think she was. I believe she was saying to enjoy the people in your life while you still have them and to not take them for granted because you never know how long you'll have them in your life. I think back and picture her singing, "Some of these days," and she was so right. I miss her every day.

"I believe we'll meet again someday." My sister Theresa said this to my daughters Missy and Shayna when she knew her time on earth was nearly over. She truly believed that there is a life beyond this one, and it didn't have anything to do with organized religion. It came from the depths of her heart that there is something eternal in all of us and that we will reunite somehow, somewhere."

"I can't see for looking." Mom always said this, and it means the more you look for an answer, the less likely you are to find it. So, the best thing to do is to relax, and when you least expect it, the answer will come to you. Don't ruminate or obsess. You'll find your answer.

"Joe Feezer, dayroom." My father Emidio said this non sequitur every so often, especially if people were getting on his nerves or messing with his mind. One day he walked over to Byberry Hospital to visit his doctor and attendant friends and heard this cryptic message on the PA system: "Joe Feezer, day room."
One of the staff members was telling a patient named Joe Feezer to come to the recreation room. When my dad jokingly said this in a deadpan

voice, it meant that he was trying to demystify mental illness, which was rare back then. He made a joke about it, not to make fun of emotional illness, but to say it should be treated like anything else in life and not be shunned or avoided. He wanted that for himself in his interactions with people.

"An idle mind is the devil's workshop" was said by just about every nun I've ever known. God forbid if any of their teenage charges frittered their time away on magazines, movies, or worse, boys. Stick your nose in a book, go for a walk in nature, help someone who needs it. Do anything but remain idle or indulge yourself in aimless pursuits; that is, unless you want Beelzebub to knock on your door and mess with your mind.

"A watched pot never boils." I often said this to my high school students when they stared at the clock, wondering when class would be over, and the bell would ring for the next class. I tried not to spend too much time dwelling on intricate points of grammar, but once in a while I had to bring up these and other sleep-inducing topics that my class needed to write well. This old saying means that if you watch for time to pass it will seem like forever until the lesson (or day) is over. So, embrace the time, grow and learn from it and the clock will take care of itself.

"I never saw so many big *goolahs (culos)* as I see on the boardwalk at the shore." Mom always pronounced *culo* (rear end) *goolah*, which made it sound extra funny when she said these words every time she strolled the boardwalk at our favorite beach in Ocean City, New Jersey. Mom always flaunted an ample derriere (as did I). I remember Miss Laura, who worked at The Royal Gardens, saying that Mom had big hips and how attractive she looked. In those days, people loved having hourglass figures highlighted by a big *culo*, but now many people prefer skinny butts. Go figure.

"You can forgive, but you can't forget." Mom often said this if we said something mean to her, like "I hate you," when we were kids. She let us know that she always forgave us, but that disrespecting her would always bring bad memories for her and that it would be hard to forget them.

"How soon we forget" was the ultimate guilt trip Mom laid on us. If a kid or grandchild didn't call for a while or visit, Mom would say this, always with a poor, pitiful pearl look on her face. It meant why did you forget about me and not make time for me?

In the next breath, Mom would be joking around, laughing, and inviting the offender to a spaghetti or roast beef feast with strawberry shortcake for dessert. All was quickly forgiven and the person who slighted her would once again be in her good graces. That's just the way she was.

"Got that rubber weasel?" was another goofy non sequitur Dad said, along with many others. It didn't make sense, but what did in life? When Dad said this to someone, they either laughed it off, pretending they knew what it meant or gave him a lost and befuddled look. Dad reveled in both reactions. Life sometimes didn't make sense, and Dad made a point of telling people that.

Appendix 3
Cherished Family Recipes

Food brings people together. We celebrate life by eating with friends and family. We come together when a loved one passes, and food gives us some measure of solace. Thinking of those we loved or lost who are now in the ever after, we cook their recipes to remember the scents, sights, and conversations we once enjoyed. Scents, more than any other senses, can bring us back and keep the memories of those we've loved and lost alive for us.

Here are some recipes that Mom made for us and for the customers at the restaurant and I've added some of my favorites too, and of course, Cliff's hot dogs. I hope you enjoy them. Feel free to add your unique touches to make these recipes your own or make them just as they are.

Main Dishes

Barbequed Pork Chops   Put   in temperatures and instructions.

listed, please.

Serve this tasty dish with baked cheese potatoes, fluffy muffins, and a salad.

Ingredients

4 thin to medium boneless pork chops (one or two per person)

½ cup BBQ sauce (with or without onions)

¼ cup ketchup

¼ cup hot water

1 Tablespoon honey

1 Tablespoon Worcestershire Sauce

Double sauce recipe if you like a lot of sauce.

Directions

Trim pork chops of fat. Brown pork chops in pork fat or a little butter on the stove. Pour barbeque sauce overall. Cover the baked dish and bake 25 minutes at 350 degrees. Uncover dish and cook 15 minutes until cooked. Be sure they're well done.

Baked Breaded Pork Chops (Better than packaged breading)

Ingredients
4 lean medium pork chops (one or two per person)
2 Tablespoons butter
¾ cup breadcrumbs (any kind you like)
Salt and pepper to taste.
Directions
Cut off excess fat from pork chops. Leave a little
Dampen chops with water and shake it off.
Bake at 425 for 35-40 minutes.

Broiled Mushroom Sandwiches

People of all ages love these fancy sandwiches. They don't take much time to prepare, and they're like nothing you've ever tasted. Serve with a salad.

Ingredients
1 cup of mayo (may use low fat)
½ teaspoon grated lemon peel (optional)
1 Tablespoon lemon juice
1Tablespoon chopped chives (optional)
½ cup grated Parmesan cheese
6-9 slices thick (cut ¾ inch) French or Italian bread (I like seeded French bread)
2 Tablespoons soft butter
10 thin slices of tomato

2 cups sliced mushrooms
Coarsely ground black pepper
Directions
Combine topping ingredients. Set aside. Lightly spread both sides of bread with butter. Place in broiler pan 4-5 inches from heat source. (Use the low setting.) Watch carefully so bread doesn't burn. Broil both sides lightly. When the second side is done, top each with a tomato slice and a sprinkling of black pepper. Then top with as many mushrooms as you want. Spread each with a generous spoonful of Parmesan topping. Return to broiler. Broil 3 min. or until lightly browned. Serve immediately. Cut the recipe in half or save some for the next day.

Cliff's Famous Hot Dogs

Cliff's deep-fried hot dogs are unique and tasty. If you don't want all the fat from deep frying, you can pan fry them for a few minutes. Cut them like Cliff did (directions for cutting follow) and then fry lightly. All the fixings, like mustard and onions,
will fall into the grooves and make your hot dog experience delicious. Try it and see if they aren't the best hot dogs, you ever ate. If you'd rather, French fry the hot dogs for a couple minutes at 350 degrees in a deep fryer and drain well.
How to cut hot dogs
Turn hot dog on one side. Make three slits (not cutting all the way through) with a sharp knife. Turn over and make three slits on the other side. Now go to the end of each hot dog and make a cross formation at both ends. And there you have it.

Doc Alex's Favorite French Fries

Allow one or more large potatoes per person. Pre-heat deep fryer with temperature indicator to 300 degrees. Place peeled and cut Russet potatoes in ice water for a few minutes. Dry potatoes thoroughly with paper towels. Lower fryer basket into hot peanut oil (if you want, use vegetable oil, but peanut oil is best for cooking fries). Cook for 5-6 minutes in deep fryer. Spread out partially cooked fries on paper towels. After a few minutes, increase heat on fryer to 400. Recook the blanched fries for another five minutes until they turn brown. Drain again. Sprinkle with salt and pepper. Repeat with each batch of potatoes. I cook them in small batches.

Fluffy Muffins

Mom served these muffins at her banquets, and people always asked for more.
Ingredients
1 cup milk
1 beaten egg
¼ cup melted shortening
2 cups flour
3 teaspoons baking powder
4 tablespoons sugar
½ teaspoon salt
Directions
Mix milk, egg, and shortening. Stir other ingredients together and mix with first mixture by hand. Don't beat. Pour batter into greased muffin pans (or use paper liners), 1/3 full. Bake in 425-degree oven 20 -25 minutes. Makes 12 muffins.

Italian Vegetable Soup (AKA Sick Soup)

I got this recipe from Mom, who figured out how her mother-in-law and my paternal grandmother, Luisa Spinelli (Nan Nan), made it. Amazingly, the soup tastes just like the one Nan-Nan made. My grandmother continued to make this main dish soup for our family when we visited her rowhouse in northeast Philly.

Mom could replicate any recipe to perfection without knowing the ingredients. She never used recipes. She always made this for us when we were sick. It worked better than chicken soup and we recovered quickly from whatever illness we had. You can serve it with or without meat. Give the meat to those who like it and skip it for those who don't. I serve it with a salad and cheese bread (To make cheese bread, soften butter and mix it with Parmesan cheese. Use French or Portuguese rolls (2 rolls with two tablespoons softened butter with cheese stirred in.) Spread cheese mixture on French bread and bake at 350 degrees until done the way you like it.)

This makes one soup recipe, which you can double. I always double it as it goes fast, or you can freeze the broth without the noodles and cook the noodles when you're ready. The noodles expand when cooking, so don't cook too many. Follow the directions on the box for cooking and cook them separately, not in the soup. Add to the soup shortly before serving.

Ingredients
Two meaty soup bones (I trim the fat).
Pack of baby carrots
1-2 pounds round stew meat cut up (Find it in your grocery).
2-3 stalks celery (No need to peel. Just wash, cut stems, and break in two, throwing away the stringy parts. You can use the leaves if you want. I don't.)
1 large, sweet onion cut in two.
One small can tomato paste
1 large can crushed tomatoes (For a double recipe, I use two or three large cans). Buy the ones that are crushed well, and not chunky, as you want a smooth broth.
1 or more Tablespoons of salt, to taste
½ teaspoon pepper or more.
Acini di Pepe pasta (San Georgio makes it).
Grated Parmesan Cheese to taste
You could use pastina or alphabet noodles instead of the Acini di Pepe noodles. Be sure they're well cooked.

To make the soup, put everything into a large pot. I use a 12-cup stainless steel enamel one. Add more water to fill the pot to about ¾ or less. Rinse out all the tomato paste and tomato cans and pour into pot. Bring to a boil. After soup comes to a boil, simmer on low 3 hrs. or more. Strain soup, in small batches using a strainer and big bowls.

Cut up any meat you think needs it, including the meat from the soup bones, cutting against the grain to make it tender. Throw away bones, celery and onion after straining. (You can leave some onion in the soup. Skim off the fat when soup stops boiling. I skim it and put it in the 'fridge. The next day, take off the solid fat and keep the broth that's left).

Serve with lots of grated Parmesan cheese as it adds just the right flavor.

Cook Acini di Pepe pasta according to directions and add to soup.

Mom's Sauce and Meatballs for Pasta, Lasagna, and Ravioli

Mom used this sauce or gravy as a base for all her Italian dishes.
Ingredients
1 tablespoon olive or vegetable oil to brown garlic
1 6 oz. can tomato paste
2 large cans crushed Italian tomatoes with basil.
1 large can plum tomatoes or diced tomatoes (If you use plum tomatoes, slice them first. The diced tomatoes are already sliced for you.)
a few sprigs of fresh basil chopped.
finely chopped garlic to taste (I use very little, half a clove), or use ¼ teaspoon garlic powder
one or two teaspoons sugar, more if you like it sweet
a teaspoon or two of olive or vegetable oil
salt and white pepper to taste (You can use black pepper, but white gives it a special taste.)
I use 1 teaspoon salt and ¼ teaspoon of white pepper)
red pepper crushed (a pinch) unless you like it hot
6 ounces mushrooms sliced thin (optional)
Directions
Sauté chopped garlic in olive oil. Be sure not to burn it, or sauce will be bitter, and it will ruin the taste of the sauce. Add tomato paste, salt, white pepper, sugar, and red pepper. Stir with a wooden spoon over low heat until blended. Now add the rest of the tomatoes, basil leaves, and mushrooms. Stir and bring to a slow boil. Turn to simmer and simmer at least an hour partially covered. If you add meatballs, cook for one hour or more. Be sure the sauce doesn't burn or stick to the pan. If you add browned sweet or hot sausage,

cook for two hours more.

Meatballs

Ingredients (Double ingredients, if you want)
4 slices American bread (I use white-wheat American bread)
Water or milk to soak bread (small amount)
1 lb. ground chuck (80% lean)
small amount fresh garlic (I use ¼ clove, finely chopped)
1 large egg
2 or more Tablespoons grated Parmesan cheese
salt and black pepper to taste
small amount (1/2 clove) garlic, chopped, or garlic powder
Directions
Soak bread in warm water, and squeeze water from each slice. If you want, cut off crusts, but it's not necessary. Mix all ingredients well with your hands in a large bowl until well blended. Roll mixture into balls.

Bake at 350 degrees for 20 minutes, turning after 10 minutes, until no longer pink. (Fry if you want, but I prefer them baked.) Drain meatballs with a paper towel. Add to sauce and cook for at least an hour. Serve with the pasta of your choice and fresh, grated cheese.

Note: When Mom made her famous lasagna, instead of putting ground meat between the layers, she added chopped cooked meatballs to give it extra flavor.

If you like sausage, brown sweet or hot sausage or a mixture of both in the oven at 350 degrees, turning after 15 minutes. You can also fry it if you'd prefer. I use the oven to brown it and drain it well before adding it to the sauce. Add the sausage to the sauce with the meatballs, and cook for another hour.

Refreshing Shrimp Salad

Here's my recipe for a quick one-dish lunch or dinner. It's easy to make and delicious.

Ingredients

1 package (5 ounces) salad greens or lettuce of your choice

1 pound cooked medium shrimp, peeled and deveined

1 large or medium can Mandarin orange segments

1 medium ripe avocado, peeled and chopped

1 cup fresh strawberries, quartered (sprinkle with sugar if not sweet enough)

1/2 cup thinly sliced green onions (optional)

Salad dressing of your choice (I prefer honey balsamic), but any kind is good.

Directions

On each of 4 serving plates, arrange salad greens, shrimp, orange, avocado, strawberries and onions. Drizzle with dressing. This was our main meal of the day, which we always have for lunch, like my grandparents did. I save a few shrimp and made shrimp salad sandwiches for dinner.

Roast Beef and Gravy

We like this roast beef on a Kaiser roll with a slice of sharp Provolone cheese and horseradish sauce (Mix a couple of tablespoons of horseradish with 8 ounces of low-fat sour cream). I serve roasted potatoes and buttered baby carrots as sides. If you like your roast beef on a platter, go for it. It makes a festive comfort food dinner.

Directions for Making a Tender Roast

Use a rump roast of 4-5 pounds. Wipe off the roast with a damp paper towel. Trim a little fat off the roast. Sprinkle roast with
salt and pepper. (Add rosemary if you like the taste.) Cook uncovered at 350 degrees for an hour. Then, after an hour, lower heat to 325 degrees after covering roast tightly with tin foil. Cover the entire roasting pan, and be sure the edges are tight. For rare, cook 15 minutes a pound; medium, 20, and 30 to 40 for well-done. We like it very well done, and allow 45 min. a pound, so adjust cooking time for the way you like it. It's best not to disturb the foil until it's done. The foil is what tenderizes the meet.

Gravy: Pour the meat drippings into a clear bowl. Let it sit and then skim off most of the fat. Pour into a saucepan and add two regular beef bouillon cubes until dissolved. Then pour a cup of water and 2 Tablespoons of flour into a shaker cup. Shake it up until it's dissolved. Add to drippings and add salt and pepper to taste. Mix with a wire whisk until smooth (3 minutes or so after it comes to a boil). If it's too thick, add water to make it a good consistency. Taste it to see if the seasonings are right.

Gravy with Gravy Mix: This is good if you like a lot of gravy. Use liquid or powdered gravy mix. Add this after following directions for preparation to the prepared gravy mix. The only kind I use is Knorr Beef Gravy Mix, mixed with my own.

Instead of making the homemade gravy, you can add beef drippings, minus the fat to the prepared gravy. Mix with a wire whisk until smooth about 3 or 4 minutes. Add more water as it gets very thick. Add more water if you need it. Let roast sit a few minutes before carving. Serve with gravy.

Roasted potatoes are a good combo with the beef. You can roast Russet potatoes along with the beef. Cut them in half or smaller. Surround the roast with the potatoes while you're cooking the beef uncovered. In about half an hour turn them so that the fat from the beef bathes them. Cook them while the beef cooks uncovered. When you cover the beef with foil, place potatoes in a pie pan or another type pan and cook separately in the oven with the beef for about an hour or so more, depending on how tender you like them. Complete the feast with boiled baby carrots with butter and dill, if you like.

Shrimp Scampi with Ponzu Sauce

Here's one of my own favorite recipes that I think Mom would have enjoyed because she loved seafood. It's quick, easy, and elegant. Serves 4.
Ingredients:
pounds large uncooked shrimp, shelled and deveined
1/2 cup butter
1 teaspoon salt
2 cloves garlic, crushed
1 teaspoon lemon zest (lemon rind grated)
2 tablespoons lemon juice
lemon wedges

Mushrooms Cut mushrooms and sauté in a smidgen of butter (as much as you want of the mushrooms)

Kikkoman Ponzu sauce (Find in grocery store or online).

Directions

Preheat oven to 400°. Peel and devein shrimp. Melt butter in a 13x9x2-inch baking pan in oven. To the melted butter, add the salt, crushed garlic, 1 Tablespoon of Kikkoman Ponzu sauce, and 1 tablespoon of the chopped parsley. Stir well. Arrange shrimp scampi in baking pan in a single layer. Bake, uncovered, for 5 minutes. Turn shrimp; sprinkle with lemon zest, lemon juice, and the rest of the parsley. Add sautéed mushrooms, distributing evenly. Bake shrimp for 5-6 minutes, or until just done. Arrange shrimp scampi on hot serving platter; pour garlic butter from pan over the shrimp and garnish with several lemon wedges, or serve over rice.

Note: I make this with one pound of shrimp and half all the ingredients for two people. If I want a lighter version for one pound of shrimp, I use two T of butter (instead of four) and 2 T of lemon juice in addition to the other lemon juice you pour over it when you turn the shrimp. I serve it over rice. When it's done, I sprinkle on a little Ponzu sauce and grating cheese.

Theresa's Salad Dressing

This is a good basic salad dressing you can use for family dinners or special occasions. Add blue or Gorgonzola cheese, white raisins, mandarin oranges, dried cherries, croutons, or any salad fixings you like.

Ingredients

2/3 cup olive oil

1/3 cup red wine vinegar

1 teaspoon liquid Dijon mustard

1 crushed garlic clove

1 teaspoon kosher salt

½ teaspoon freshly ground pepper

1 teaspoon oregano

½ teaspoon dried basil

½ teaspoon dried parsley

Shake or mix together and pour on greens of your choice. I like to add blue or Gorgonzola cheese to it, along with dried cherries and white raisins. It's good plain too.

Side Dishes

Baked Stuffed Cheese Potatoes

Bake or microwave 4 large baked potatoes.
Ingredients
4 large potatoes
½ cup green onion or sweet onion (1 Tablespoon)
½ cup grated Parmesan
½ cup sour cream
2 Tablespoons butter
Bake potatoes in oven or microwave. Let cool a few minutes. Cut in two. Scoop out top only. Mix all ingredients by hand with potato masher or in mixer. Re-bake in potato skins at for thirty minutes in 350 degree oven until browned.

Broccoli Casserole

Mom's recipe is different from most in that she didn't add mayonnaise like most do. I think it makes all the difference. I usually make half and freeze half.
Ingredients
1 can cream of mushroom soup (may use low salt or low fat)
3 tablespoons sour cream
2-4 tablespoons white cheddar
Stir soup, sour cream and cheddar in a small bowl
2 tablespoons melted butter
¾ -1 cup breadcrumbs (you can use cheese breadcrumbs if you want.)
One head broccoli trimmed and cut up, or use 1 16 oz. package of frozen chopped broccoli, cooked.
Directions

Put trimmed and chopped or frozen cooked broccoli in 13 by 9 pan. Mix butter and breadcrumbs in a shallow pan and stir. Pour mixture with soup on top. Sprinkle with buttered breadcrumbs. Bake at 350 degrees until browned and bubbling.

Dessert

Mom's Orange Cake

Mom served this festive cake often. If you want, garnish with thin orange slices.

Ingredients

1 box vanilla butter cake mix

Substitute orange juice for water.

Dash of grated orange cake.

Bake cake as directed on cake mix box.

Orange Butter Frosting

Ingredients

4 Tablespoons butter

4 Tablespoons solid shortening (not buttery flavored)

1 lb. box powdered sugar

1 teaspoon vanilla extract

4-6 Tablespoons orange juice (enough to make it the right consistency)

3 Tablespoons orange rind grated thin

1 box (16 oz.) confectioner's sugar

Instructions

Beat all ingredients at slow speed until blended. Then beat at high speed until smooth and creamy.

Butter Icing for any kind of cake

Mom always said that shortening cuts the sweetness of frosting made with butter. Here's the easy recipe.

Ingredients for Vanilla Icing

4 Tablespoons softened butter

4 Tablespoons vegetable shortening

1 box (16 oz.) confectioner's sugar

1 tablespoon vanilla extract
2 or more tablespoons milk or cream
1 -2 T vanilla extract
For chocolate icing, add two or more tablespoons cocoa (not instant).
Instructions
Mix all ingredients well in mixer. Start out on slow speed and move up to high

Also by the Author
at
Rogue Phoenix Press

A Place of Learning
A Teacher's Story

Imagine what it would be like if you could see everything that goes on during one teacher's day. A Place of Learning: A Teacher's Story, a fictionalized account based on my experiences in three city high schools, spans three decades. Those who have read the book tell me the anecdotes are outrageous, poignant, funny, and sad all at the same time. Best of all, the book comes off as wild and quirky. Events similar to those in my story continue to play out every day in urban classrooms across the nation. The players are different, but the events remain the same: violence, teenage pregnancy, drug addiction, and rampant academic failure due to lack of school funding, pervasive poverty, and dysfunctional families.

Elliot K. Carnucci is a Big Fat Loser
A Book About Bullying

The kids at Ralph Bunche Middle School love to pick on Elliot Kravitz-Carnucci. He struggles with his weight, looks like a geek, makes top honors, and lives above the Carnucci Home for Funerals in South Philadelphia with his distant, workaholic father and Nonna, his quirky, overbearing grandmother. Since his parents divorced, he splits his time between living with his father and his mother Rayna, who dreams of becoming the queen of commercials, on the west coast. At the hands of his peers, Elliot experiences a series of bullying episodes that escalate from entrapment in a school supply closet to a brutal "swirly" (head dunk in the toilet) that lands him in the hospital emergency room. Can Elliot win his fight against the nasty bullies, or is he doomed forever? Read this funny, sad, and crazy book to find out.

About the Author

Catherine DePino sold twenty-two books for parents, teachers, and children to mainstream publishers. Her background includes a Bachelor's in English and Spanish education, a Master's in English education, and a doctorate in Curriculum Theory and Development and Educational Administration from Temple University. The author worked for many years as a teacher, department head of English and world languages, disciplinarian, and curriculum writer in the Philadelphia School District. After this, she worked at Temple as an adjunct assistant professor and student teaching supervisor. She is also a certified psychic by Kyle Grey, master teacher. Catherine has written articles for national magazines, including *The Christian Science Monitor* and *The Writer*. She also served on the board of The Philadelphia Writers' Conference.